BELIEFS OF A UNITED METHODIST CHRISTIAN

BY
EMERSON COLAW

tidings

1908 Grand Ave., Nashville, Tennessee, 37203

Library of Congress Card Catalog Number: 7295656
Copyright © 1972 by Tidings, 1908 Grand Avenue,
Nashville, Tennessee 37203

CONTENTS

PREFACE

This book presents the efforts of one local pastor, who served on the Theological Study Commission on Doctrine and Doctrinal Standards of The United Methodist Church, to relate the Doctrinal Statement to his own parish life.

The material in each chapter formed the basis for a sermon which was preached to the congregation. Following this kind of exposure the congregation was invited to study the Doctrinal Statement in small groups. At the time of writing, this process is under way and appears to be a fruitful method of study, reflection, and Christian growth.

The aim of this present effort in printed form is to stimulate other pastors, congregations, and individuals to become involved in the task of theologizing within United Methodist tradition. To take this task seriously could lead The United Methodist Church to a great awakening of the spirit-filled and spirit-lead life.

This volume is designed to be read, pondered, and discussed. Finally, it is to be used as one reference in hammering out one's own theological position and understanding. The reader is invited into dialogue with the author with the hope that new insight and new understanding will emerge.

1
PLURALISM

A seminary professor once remarked to a group of preachers, "Never let me hear you say you are not a theologian! As you preach and teach in the local church, you are the theologian in residence." This is a difficult image for some of us to accept. Yet every pastor, and possibly every layman, has encountered the question, "What does your church believe?" The answer has usually been what one particular United Methodist believes, but we have attempted to answer. There is no escaping the necessity to speak of convictions and beliefs, emphases and directions, which we hold in common. At the same time, we must recognize that within our denomination there is a bewildering array of doctrinal diversity. "Pluralism is a major tenet," affirms the 1972 Doctrinal Statement.

Within this pluralism, however, there is a core of truth which we affirm along with other Christian people. The sovereignty of God, the revelation of God in Jesus Christ, the continuing activity of God in the world as the Holy Spirit, the uniqueness of Scripture, the reality of the redeemed life, and the call to servanthood are essentials which we gladly proclaim. Yet there is a willingness to think and let think, as long as beliefs are tested by experience, Scripture, reason, and tradition.

There is no creed to which every United Methodist must pledge allegiance. We honor the Apostles' Creed and the other expressions that are to be found in the hymnal. These are valued liturgical assets as well as aids in our teaching ministry. But there is no theological party-line in our denomination to which all must subscribe. If such were to happen, it would tend to discourage further theological inquiry and make us static, fixed, and unable to respond to the new dimensions each generation brings. We therefore accept, as a part of our distinctive style, the fact that words such as diversity, pluralism, renewalist, evangelical, and new theologies are a part of our vocabulary as United Methodists.

This concept of pluralism and diversity is as old as the church. The men who followed Jesus were a mixed lot. Their inclinations and interests differed. There is rich variety in the way they told the gospel story indicating that the guiding Divine Spirit has respect for the individuality and special purpose of the respective writers. Furthermore, because each man discovered the Christ in his own experience this influenced the way in which he understood the life of Jesus and the relation he bore to human salvation.

The masses of people who met Jesus and were touched by him were not a homogenized crowd. They were shepherds and magi, taxgatherers and farmers, children and the influential, blind beggars and generous women, in fact, representatives of every class in society and of every type conceivable in the moral order. The beautiful thing to note is that our Lord came to each one in the way that person could receive him. This principle of diversity and pluralism continued after his death and resurrection.

At the time of Pentecost we are told that, ". . . there were staying in Jerusalem Jews of deep faith from every nation of the world . . . and they were completely bewildered because each one of them heard . . . in his own language." The Good News about the living power of the Risen Christ came to them in the way they could grasp it. Pentecost is usually associated with the coming of the Holy Spirit but it is also a symbol of the Spirit's power to overcome disunity.

This oneness in diversity is expressed by the Apostle Paul in 1 Corinthians 12 when he says: "Men have different gifts, but it is the same Spirit that gives them. There are different ways of serving God, but it is the same Lord who is served; God works through different men in different ways, but it is the same God who achieves his purpose through them all. Each man is given his gift by the Spirit that he may use it for the common good." This is an appropriate passage for us. Just as the Apostle Paul was persuaded that God works through different persons in different ways, one of the assets of a church such as ours is the infinite variety of styles, persons, and commitments that compose our constituency.

What a multiform church is the United Methodist! We should notice our differences, glory in them, and desire above all else to preserve them. We do not want—do we?—a homogeneous church where we "water everyone down" to a common point of view. We desire—don't we?—concrete variety? In Virgil Sexton's book, *Listening to the Church*, he reports from a conference in New England which says: "We should respect all cultures. This is not to say that we should ever be a 'melting pot' for all . . . we affirm diversity as a value to be maintained." (p. 52).

Dr. Dan Poling tells about trying to entertain his children one day by telling them the story of their family. He said to them, "Geographically we Polings are very representative. Your mother was born in the midwest, I was born in Oregon. Some of you were born in Ohio, one in Massachusetts, and one in New York." Little Jane, who had been listening very intently, spoke up and said, "Isn't it wonderful how we all got together?"

Well, we got together: east and west, black and white,

fundamentalist and liberal, pietist and social activist, and fortunately we are learning that our church is big enough to make room for all of us with our differing theological and ideological points of view. We are learning that we can hear the Word of God in our own individual language. We don't all have to do and say it the same way. In fact, our multiplicity becomes a virtue. Kahlil Gibran, the Lebanese poet, suggests this in his thoughts about marriage when he said:

> Sing and dance together and be joyous, but let each
> one of you be alone, even as the strings of a lute
> are alone though they quiver with the same music.
> And stand together, yet not too near together: for
> the pillars of the temple stand apart, and the oak
> tree and the cypress grow not in each other's
> shadow.

If all the pillars of the temple were pushed to one corner, the building would collapse. Standing apart, each with its own responsibility, there is symmetry, strength, service. "Let the pillars of the temple stand apart!"

We accept this principle of pluralism because we have discovered that truth has a better chance when there is diversity. Heresy is taking a fragment of the truth and giving it an emphasis beyond its actual significance. Truth has more opportunity when there is a tension between opposing positions. All great virtues are the results of two moral forces pulling in opposite directions. Love degenerates unless it is balanced by the capacity for righteous indignation. Renewal and vitality result from cross-polarization of different positions. Constructively used, disagreements and conflicts lead to growth. We are stretched to better understanding and clearer articulation of what we believe.

Mr. Sexton, in his book, said that he constantly heard comments urging the denomination to make differences authentic; to keep those who differ in communication with each other and thus learning from each other. When we do this, polarization ceases to be detrimental and becomes an aid in the search for truth. By its very nature Christianity is divisive. It forces people to choose sides on issues. In fact, the only kind of issue that doesn't polarize people is the kind that doesn't matter one way or another. John says that Jesus caused a "split among the people." Once we take a position, however, there is the temptation to become insulated, closed, and insensitive to other aspects of the issue. When this happens, truth dies! Truth is too variegated to be cribbed and caged in one set of affirmations. We need to rub our ideas and understandings against those held by others even though this irritates and makes us feel vulnerable and threatened. As Paul suggests, in a healthy body we listen to each other, respect each other, and, incidentally, may be saved from giving ourselves to positions that in time prove to be ludicrous.

It has been my privilege to serve as a member of the Theological Commission on Doctrine and Doctrinal Standards for the quadrennium of 1968-1972. It was felt that because of the tremendous variety of beliefs among United Methodists, we needed a new doctrinal statement. It was quickly decided that we could not develop a creed to which all in our church must give adherence. The Commission even found it impossible to agree, for there were theologians and pastors and laymen who represented every sequence of the theological spectrum. We decided that doctrine could not be a legalistic nor juridical standard for excommunication or censure. All we could do was speak with assurance of emphases and directions which we hold in common and then let each board, each person, hammer out his own understanding of his faith and task.

To those who belong to the Confessional denominations, our approach must seem inefficient and chaotic. The value of our doctrinal style is that our theologizing takes place within a situation of doctrinal diversity which produces fruitful tension.

This can lead us to understand our faith in such a way that it will stimulate each of us to vital worship and celebration, significant evangelistic outreach, and meaningful social and missional application.

The secretary of our Theological Commission said that within broadly defined limits United Methodists are commended to hold in creative tension all of the new and old religious thoughts and movements; the Jesus Freaks, neo-fundamentalism, Pentecostalism, and the new humanism and new process theology as well as the trends of our times such as the theology of politics and liberation for women, blacks, minority groups, and youth. We are commended to have a clearer look, and to listen more intently to the cries of each such group and its enunciation of the gospel! In this way we are confident truth has a better chance of being discovered.

We also accept the principle of pluralism because differing styles of worship, of theological statement, and of flexibility in program are needed if we are to serve the interests of the varied groups and ages that compose our membership. There is no longer any such thing as only one congregation in the local church. There are many congregations. Many life styles and theological commitments are in as well as out of the church. And this requires a variety of resource materials.

Someone has pointed out that General Motors will never make the mistake of offering only one model for its constituency with the implied attitude, "Buy it or walk." And we can't take the attitude, "If you don't like the way we say things, go somewhere else."

The pastor of Community Church in Columbus, Ohio, who was once known for his interest in small groups recently said that he has discovered that some people can't function well in that kind of setting, so church life today should have all kinds of pursuits, interests, concerns, and developmental stages.

"I see the church as a pilgrim people on the way, a traveling

group with people coming and going. . . . In our church,"
he continued, "things have broken open. One group is concerned with poverty, others are concerned with housing, with
healing, with theological study. . . . In our situation it seems
right to try to recognize the great diversity of our family!"

There is, of course, a danger. It is the temptation to assume
that the enemy is not the rampant evil in the world but the
fellow who differs from me. Within our denomination we now
have caucus groups where like-minded persons gather to discuss
their beliefs. I do not view this as a negative development.
It has brought involvement and participation on the part of
many who formerly were passive. It has garnered information
and clarified issues. Unfortunately, it can be destructive and
injurious to the Body of Christ if these worthy objectives are
lost in the effort to outmaneuver some other interest-group.
The faithful churchman will always ask himself probing questions about why he is taking his position. It is possible that
it is to provide for neurotic ego-needs that have little to do
with faithful obedience.

A book of some years ago, *Apostles in Discord*, written by
a Methodist minister, grew out of a doctoral thesis submitted
at Columbia University and Union Theological Seminary. It
is a survey of groups and individuals, most of them on the
fringes of Protestantism, who promote hate and disruption. The
ministry of hate incites hostility toward minority groups. The
ministry of disruption spearheads reckless assaults upon the
ecumenical movement and defames church leaders who believe
the message of Christianity should spur us to work for social
improvement. This is the dangerous aspect of our pluralism.
It can splinter and fragment until the unity of the Body of
Christ is lost. But we take the risk in order that we may reap
the rewards of a vital church, alive with ferment and dialogue,
sometimes moving off in all directions, but illustrating so richly
the truth of Paul's assertion that there are different gifts, dif-

ferent ways of serving God, but it is the same God who achieves his purpose through them all.

The president of Hebrew Union College, in a recent address, said that some Jews wish to deny their Jewishness or say, "I'm Reformed," or, "I'm Orthodox." "But when Moses led the Israelites from Egyptian bondage," he reminded his audience, "every Jew was there. When Joshua possessed the promised land, every Jew was there. When they were led into dispersion, and then came back to rebuild the city, every Jew was there. When the concentration camps with their gas ovens were built, every Jew was there. When the dream and longing of the centuries was fulfilled, and Israel was established again— reclaiming a barren country, planting the vineyards and groves, every Jew was there!"

In similar fashion, we can remind ourselves, when John Wesley wrote to George Shadford saying, "I turn you loose on the great continent of America. Publish your message in the open face of the sun and do all the good you can," every United Methodist was there. When Otterbein, and three others, joined in laying their hands on Francis Asbury's head, thus consecrating him as a bishop, every United Methodist was there. When G. Bromley Oxnam took his lonely, courageous stand before the Congressional Committee, which at that time was subverting its proper responsibility by engaging in witch-hunting, every United Methodist was there. When E. Stanley Jones writes *The Way*, a book of faith and vision, every United Methodist is in it. We have a rich diversity and pluralism in heritage, doctrine, and present practice that constitutes not a threat but a promise. Our controversy, our debating, our varied styles and emphases, our probing and seeking, reflect a healthy body. We are not necessarily one in doctrine, but we are one in hope—that the kingdoms of this world shall become the kingdom of our Christ. And through it all there is, as Paul phrased it, ". . . the operation of the same Spirit."

2
GOD

The statement on Doctrine adopted by the 1972 General Conference of the United Methodist Church affirms that all valid Christian doctrine is born from our response in faith to the wondrous mystery of God's love in Jesus Christ as recorded in Scripture. With all other Christian bodies we acknowledge belief in the triune God—Father, Son, and Holy Spirit. The statement also reminds us that the theological substance of our heritage begins with the biblical witness to God's reality as Creator and to his gracious self-involvement in the dramas of history. We shall examine "his gracious self-involvement in the dramas of history" in the chapters on Jesus Christ and the Holy Spirit. In this chapter we begin with a consideration of our most basic belief which is that of God as Creator.

Rarely has there been a time when more questions are being raised about our faith in God. A phrase widely heard in the decade of the sixties was "Christian Atheism." This meant that you accepted the life and teachings of Jesus, and were inspired by them, but it was impossible to say that God existed. One professor wrote that the idea of God is too exalted for the concept of existence to apply. But looked at in the cold light of day, and stripped of all ambiguities, this kind of talk is really atheism and should be so identified.

Then there has been the cult of antisupernaturalism. You will remember the phenomenally popular book *Honest to God*. The author began by trying to debunk the idea of "God out there" for there is no triple-decker universe. Now we realize that if he were right, God is limited to the natural order and to whatever is in human experience. He was not saying that he did not believe in God, but that he did not believe in God in a supernatural sense.

The problem is the ancient one of inward and outward—immanence and transcendence. By immanence we mean the indwelling of the divine world; by transcendence we mean that the divine reality is not limited to our natural order. Historically, basic Christianity has stressed both immanence and transcendence, but confusion has come in our time by the virtual denial of transcendence. The person who believes that God is merely "in here" is departing significantly from the witness of Christ, who in his most personal prayer addressed the Father as "Lord of Heaven and Earth," thus including both sides of the divine character.

The third major attack on the specifically Christian conception of God in our generation has been that of impersonalism. Christ, we know, approached the Father in a thoroughly personal fashion, especially in his prayers. But countless contemporary men and women have been convinced that they cannot, with intellectual respectability, follow Christ in this regard. The chief instrument of their attack has been a use of the word "anthropomorphic," which merely means "after the fashion of a man." They are told that if they employ the metaphor "father" and think of God as a person, they are falling back into childish ways. When we say that God is a person, someone is likely to ask, "Do you really believe God is a big man up in the sky?" We must remember, however, that the only genuine alternative to "personal" is "impersonal" and if God is nothing but "Life Force," "Eternal Values," or "Moral Law" we have cut the nerve of vital faith.

Some of the questions raised by the theological inquiry of recent years were necessary and helpful. When we heard the phrase, "God is dead," we realized that some of our notions about God were inadequate and should be allowed to die. Many were forced to recognize that God no longer existed as a Living Reality in their lives. Dr. Harold Bosley, of Christ Church, New York, was taking part in a meeting of the World Council of Churches. He was interviewed by a reporter and Dr. Bosley assumed he would ask what the Council was going to say about some pressing world problem. But the reporter asked about the "death of God" by saying, "Is God really dead?" And Dr. Bosley asked, "What difference would it make to you, personally, this very minute if I should answer, 'Yes, God is dead' "? The reporter changed the subject. For him, however, it was apparent that God was dead.

Most of us, however, find our faith shaken not by radical theologians but by the hard facts of life. There was the young woman who said, "I've watched four members of my family die with cancer. Surely you don't expect me to believe in a personal God who loves us and cares for us!" One can understand Hugh Walpole making a young man in one of his novels exclaim, "You know there can't be a God, Vanessa. In your heart you must know it. You are a wise woman. You read and think. Well, ask yourself, 'How can there be a God and life be as it is?' " Echoing this sentiment was the young university professor who commented, "I can't believe in God, although I sometimes wish I did." He is representative of a vast number who are troubled, feel doubt and confusion, are often inclined to resist the declarations of the church, and yet basically yearn for a vital faith. In an effort to be helpful, we might profit from an examination of what we mean by a belief in "God's reality as Creator" and "his gracious self-involvement in the dramas of history."

Consider, for a moment, the traditional arguments for the existence of God. There is the argument from cause and effect. Every effect must have its cause. There is the argument from life. Man can alter, develop, rearrange, but he cannot create life. He transmits it, but life is a gift. If it is a gift, then this implies a giver. There is the argument from design. When we discover a world where there is order, where tides ebb and flow and where the planets never leave their courses, we are bound to say: "I have found a world. Somewhere there must be a world-maker." There is the moral argument. The very word "ought" implies a standard given from beyond the human situation, and sanctions imposed by a power above. Then some find credence in the idea of the universal belief in God. There has never been discovered a tribe of men who did not pray.

Finally, there is the argument of experience. Through the centuries men of the highest reputation and of the strongest character have been convinced that in this universe there is a power other than human power. They base this conviction on the reality of their own experience. They are quite sure that God spoke to them in guidance and comfort, and in looking back they are confident they can trace the guiding hand of God. They would say that the presence of God is the most real thing in the world. There are those, however, who do not find these conclusive.

A young graduate student said that in college he came in contact with a picture of the universe that was much more convincing than the Bible. It was, he said, built on real knowledge, on facts that have been tested scientifically. We make no claim for the biblical traditions of creation as scientific documents. It is abundantly clear that the writers of the creation story in Genesis were not interested in *When* and *What* and *How* but *Who* and *Why*.

The study of science is a proper task for man. God created us with curiosity. We seek answers. We want to know how things happened. However, there is a word of caution. Remember, science is not the only avenue to truth. It is neutral and deals with very limited aspects of reality. Furthermore, the confirmed generalizations of all sciences admit that there need be no conflict between the sciences and a belief in a personal God, as some would suggest. We do not attack science, we are grateful for its contribution. But we do believe humility from the scientist for his field is not the final arbiter of truth. When we hear someone say, in referring to the biblical account of creation, "It couldn't have happened that way," or, "I don't believe in miracles," then we know they are out of touch with the possible.

A science magazine carried an important debate by reputable authorities on how the earth got here and where man came from. The conclusion: "We don't know. We have a lot of interesting theories—but we don't know." A few school systems are experimenting with the use of optional materials in talking about creation—including the Bible. At a meeting of the American Association for the Advancement of Science, John Moore, a professor of natural science at Michigan State, read a paper charging that evolution is a "religion" but not a science: "It is worth discussion and investigation," he said, "but more and more the results of disciplined experimentation fail to conform to what would be expected if Darwinism were true."

It is not our wish, however, to engage in the old debate of science versus revelation. Our purpose is to proclaim those basic beliefs which grasp us as United Methodists. And we are, in the first place, persuaded that an orderly world affirms a Creator.

Our lives depend upon a dependable world. We measure our lives by the regular movement of the sun and the earth on which we live. The stability of our buildings, the power of our atomic energy, and the speed of our planes are all expressions of the regularity in the nature of things.

Now how did this orderly world get here? It didn't happen by chance. We know in our own lives that when anything is orderly and dependable, behind it is an engineering mind. The trustworthy, reliable operations of our man-made world, our technology, are utterly dependent upon the order imposed by and utilized by the creative, ordering minds of men. On the basis of our experience, we must know that the presence of dependability in the universe implies the operation of an ordering principle.

W. McFerrin Stowe relates that scientist A. Cressy Morrison, in a simple illustration, has shown the improbability of chance in a universe of such perplexity. If you were to place ten coins in your pocket, numbered one through ten, the chance of drawing them out in succession would be one in ten billion. He concludes: "So many essential conditions are necessary for life to exist on our earth that it is impossible that all of them could exist in proper relationship by chance. Therefore, there must be in nature some form of intelligent direction."

Furthermore, Mr. Morrison has pointed out that the earth is tilted at 23.5 degrees. If it were tilted more or less, life as we know it could not exist—but it is tilted exactly at 23.5 degrees. What a mind it took to plan the earth so there would be daylight and dark, land and sea, summer and winter, seedtime and harvest, animals and plants, rain and sunshine.

Our world is full of wonders that defy any rational explanation and call for the presence of a great and all-powerful Creative Mind. Consider the story of the monarch butterflies. These tiny, fragile members of God's creation, weighing little more than a bird's feather, fly hundreds of miles to spend the winter in warmer climates. The flocks of butterflies that span the North American continent and arrive in late October at

Pacific Grove, California, have long been famous. An estimated two million monarchs spend the winter, year after year, on the same trees in a six-acre area. The most spectacular feature of their migration is that they gather on these same trees each year. Their life span is so short, no butterfly could possibly make the round trip twice. How then, do they find their way over such great distances? There is only one answer: God has provided compass and direction!

Observe the care with which the mother wasp provides for her children. When the mother wasp has laid her eggs, she stings a grasshopper in exactly the right spot so that he does not die but is completely paralyzed, living as a kind of preserved meat. She then drags the grasshopper to where the eggs are, flies away and dies, never setting eyes on her eggs again. When the eggs finally hatch, the baby wasps have their food supply in the form of instant grasshopper right at hand. Now, all this is an enormously complicated process; there is no margin for error, and the first mother wasp who set this process in motion had to do it perfectly, or today there would be no wasps.

As you reflect upon this, you realize that the mother wasp has been endowed with a marvelous set of instincts to take care of her children. You reason back from these instincts to the creative force in the universe, and you conclude that the wasp—and indeed, the whole natural order—must be the work of a Supreme Intelligence.

Another demonstration of this idea is the silver eel. According to the Encyclopedia Britannica, these lowly fish come from all over the world to the Gulf Stream off Bermuda. In autumn, when they are ready to lay their eggs, they swim out from the fresh-water streams of Europe and this continent into the ocean, and come to this one spot. Having given birth to their young, they die. Then in the spring the newborn eels go back to the same rivers from whence their mothers came. How do they know to do this?

These incidents out of nature illustrate the need for an organizing intelligence which stands both above and within this universe. Dr. Robert Jasrow gave a series of television lectures on "The New Science." He used the word "accident" a number of times. "Various stages of development," he said, "were the result of an accident—a happenstance." This is as difficult to accept intellectually as the biblical notion of six days! God is a God of order. Chaos is anti-God!

The second affirmation, however, is more difficult. The Christian faith proclaims that this Creative Impulse is aware of itself, is a person. Again, we must base our conviction not only upon the Scripture but also upon our own experience.

In this world, we say, man is distinct in that he is aware of himself, examines and tries to understand himself. If man is self-aware, then the ultimate nature of reality must include the personal. Chester Pennington illustrates this in the following way: when a wife brings chocolate cake to the dinner table, remarking that she baked it from scratch, we must assume that in the universe which produced it (her kitchen) there existed the ingredient of chocolate. It cannot appear if it does not exist. So when self-awareness appears in man, it must have already existed. That which is highest in ourselves is a reflection of that which is deepest in the universe!

In other words, as human intelligence implies the existence of intelligence in the very nature of things, so human personality implies the existence of personality at the very core of reality. We are moved to conclude that not only is there a Creative Intelligence in this universe, but this Organizing Power is a Person with self-awareness. In this sense, while God and man belong to two utterly different orders, there is an affinity between them which was brought about by God himself. They both have self-awareness and are both persons!

The third affirmation held by United Methodists about God is that while he is beyond man he is also for man. He is for man because he created him in his own image (Genesis 1:27). The earliest historian of note in the British Isles was the venerable Bede. It was he who wrote of a man who described life as the flight of a sparrow out of darkness across a lighted banquet hall into darkness. Many might find this an apt description. They would have difficulty with Wordsworth's idea expressed in his ode on "Intimations of Immortality" when he wrote: "But trailing clouds of glory do we come, from God, who is our home." We believe that God created man out of his own nature, for a purpose, and he does not despise but cherishes what he himself has made.

In his relationships with his creature, man, God has placed two limitations upon himself. He is limited by the structure of his creation. If this world is to be reasonable and intelligent, then it must be subject to the orderliness to which we have referred. I must not expect God to periodically intervene and upset the natural course of events in my behalf. If he were to do that, even once, then he could be guilty of being capricious, of saving some and not others.

We often assume that if God is love he will exercise a discriminatory power for us. We do not want him to make the sun to rise on the just and the unjust but to reserve it for the just. We plead, "Why did this happen to me? I go to church every Sunday?" Does this mean that the laws of aging in which vital human organs wear out should not apply to us? Does this mean that the laws of this universe are to be set aside for us so that if we fall we are not injured as others? Some years ago eighty-seven children and three teachers were killed in a parochial school fire in Chicago. In a television interview following the tragedy, a clergyman called it "the will of God." What a frightful thing to say. If God plots such tragedies, why should we bother with building codes, safety regulations, and fire escapes? And why bother with God?

Leslie Weatherhead in his helpful volume on the will of

God tells of visiting a friend in India during an epidemic. The friend's son died. The two men were walking on the veranda of the home. At the far end of the porch a tiny girl, the only remaining child, lay asleep under a mosquito net. The father said, "Well, Reverend, it's the will of God."

Knowing the man intimately, and wanting to help him think through the implications of this comment, Weatherhead replied, "Suppose someone crept up the steps onto the veranda tonight while you all slept, and deliberately put a wad of cotton soaked in cholera germ culture over your little girl's mouth as she lay there . . . what would you think about that?"

"My God," the father cried, "I'd kill him with as little feeling as I would a snake."

"But John," Weatherhead said, "isn't that just what you've accused God of doing when you said it was his will? Call your little boy's death the result of mass ignorance, call it mass folly, call it mass sin . . . but don't call it the will of God."

This point of view may raise questions as to the meaning of intercessory prayer. A later discussion will consider this matter. The only point we are now trying to make is that God has created a dependable universe. The Christian is as subject to the laws of this world as the next person. Prayer is concerned with matters other than trying to get God to do what he ordinarily would not do.

God also limits himself by the reality of human freedom. We are not automatons. He set us free in this world so that through joy and sorrow, success and failure, we are free to become genuine persons, molding our own lives. Often it is asked why God allows men to make war, to build slums, and to create the injustices that abound. But to ask why God does not stop war, or why he allows exploitations and slums is to ask why God does not stop being God. Because he is a God of love, he will not treat his creature-man as less than a free human being, who must learn and grow and come at last to full maturity, through suffering and travail perhaps, but who will be a spiritual personality rather than an automatic machine.

Jesus told a matchless story in which he said God was like a father. A father does not shut us in a room away from danger. He permits us to mature through experience, to use our freedom even though it carries a risk. And a real father, while he may not always be able to keep us from danger, suffers with us while we go through the difficult experience. For the Christian, this is part of the meaning of Christ, who "reflects the glory of God and bears the very stamp of his nature. . . ." (Hebrews 1:3)

In spite of these limitations which God places upon himself, we still affirm that he is *for* man, that he loves us with an everlasting love. A former governor of Wyoming, Milward Simpson, in a devotional article, tells of flying in a plane that developed trouble. When the pilot announced they were going to try an unscheduled emergency landing, the governor took the hand of his wife and together they offered a simple statement of faith they often shared:

> The light of God surrounds us,
> The love of God enfolds us,
> The power of God protects us,
> And the presence of God watches over us;
> Wherever we are, God is.

Then he added that they knew the asserting of this affirmation would not make everything turn out all right. Rather, saying what they said was their way of declaring the confidence that "living or dying, we are in his care." This is what we mean when we say, "God is *for* us."

A young woman came to her pastor with a question, "How can I believe that God is interested in what happens to me?"

He answered, "Look at your fingers. There are billions of finger-tips in the world, but no others are like yours. Even your fingertips have had special attention from God." Then he instructed her, "Whenever you doubt, look at your hand-carved fingertips and know that God is interested in you personally."

In this chapter we have been talking about our faith in God. He is the source of life, the One in whom we live, move, and have our being. It is well that we remember his greatness. At the funeral of Louis XIV, the cathedral was filled with mourners who had come to pay their final tribute to the King, whom they all considered to be great. The room was dark, save for one lone candle illuminating the gold casket which held the mortal remains of the monarch. At the appointed time, the Court Preacher stood to address the citizens. As he rose he reached from his pulpit and snuffed out the one candle which had been put there alone to symbolize the greatness of the King. Then from the darkness came just four words, "God only is great."

3
CHRIST

In an earlier chapter reference was made to the "theological pluralism" which characterizes our denomination. We suggested our doctrinal stance includes an awareness of the transcendent mystery of divine truth which allows us in good conscience to acknowledge the positive virtues of doctrinal pluralism even within the same community of believers. In this we are following what Wesley called "catholic spirit" which also prevails in much contemporary ecumenical theology. We can heartily endorse the classical ecumenical watchword: "In essentials, unity; in nonessentials, liberty; and in all things, charity" (love that cares and understands).

The Doctrinal Statement of our General Conference also recognized that the ecumenical process has expanded across the boundaries of Christian unity, to include serious interfaith encounters and explorations between Christianity and other living religions of the world. We must now be conscious that God has been and is now working among all people. There is a new sense in which we realize that we are given to each other on this fragile small planet, to work out with God the salvation, health, healing, and peace he intends for all his people. In these less familiar encounters, however, our aims are not to reduce doctrinal differences to some lowest common denominator or religious agreement, but to raise all such relationships to the highest possible level of human fellowship and understanding.

In fact, the Doctrinal Statement of 1972 affirmed that theological pluralism must not be confused with "theological indifferentism"—the notion that there are no essential doctrines and that differences in theology, when sincerely held, need no further discussion.

We are Christians because we believe there is something unique and distinctive about Christianity. We are persuaded that in the midst of our condition of need and alienation, God's unfailing grace shows itself in his suffering love working for our redemption and that the Gospels describe this fact in a way that is not recorded elsewhere.

United Methodists believe we have a faith of incomparable power and beauty which we should cherish and increasingly understand. Many in our own household, however, view it as commonplace. Intrigued by tantalizing reports of foreign faiths, some of our own youth are going to India to meditate under the guidance of a Guru or they turn to such mystical religions as Zen Buddhism for satisfaction. For their sake, and to engage meaningfully in interfaith dialogue, we must be prepared to answer the question, "Why Christianity of all religions?"

We speak from a stance of humility. We acknowledge that most of us are what we are because of birth. Furthermore, in contemporary missions the approach is dialogical. The missionary does not come in arrogance saying, "I have the truth and I will now share it with you who are benighted." He says, "I have something to learn; I have something to offer."

Nevertheless, there are two assumptions we must reject. Under the guise of tolerance we sometimes say: "All religions are equally true. It doesn't make any difference what you

believe as long as you are sincere." A man of science would
never say that. If you go to a doctor you want from him more
than sincerity. An engineer would not say that. If you board
an airplane, you want the pilot not only to be sincere but
to know there are some laws in nature you do not violate
with impunity.

In our modern culture we have exalted to an astonishing
degree the conception of broadmindedness. In the area of
religion this finds expression in the claim that Christianity is
only one of several great world religions and Jesus Christ is
only one of a number of great religious teachers. We must
reject this misconceived tolerance. All religions are not equally
true. Some of the most dastardly acts of human history have
been perpetrated in the name of religion! In the name of
religion widows have been killed and buried with their hus-
bands. In the name of religion a devout mother in India has
been known to take her cherished child to the Ganges River
and throw him into the water as a sacrifice to the gods. In
the name of religion some of our forebears in New England
destroyed certain members of the community because they were
suspected of being witches. The hearty relativism that one man's
religion is as good as another man's is fuzzy thinking and does
not stand up before the facts.

Another misconception is found in the phrase: "We're all
going to the same place; we're just taking different roads."
This phrase is acceptable if it means that denominational labels
are not very important. The proposition, however, that all the
major world religions are so many different ways to the same
goal breaks down before the facts. The Buddhist believes that
the thirst for life, the desire for this unreal world, give rise
to suffering. His goal is to find the way to Nirvana, which
is total discontinuance or extinction. The follower of Mo-
hammed may have as his goal the joys of paradise where he
can enjoy to the full the sensuous delights of the flesh. In

Christianity our goal is to be set free from the power of sin, from bondage to the powers which rule over us from within so that we are able to give ourselves to the true service of God, for in obedience to him we find our highest joy. Tolerance, unfortunately, is often another name for indifference. Neutrality usually means spiritual and mental paralysis. We reject these even as we search for real communication among the world religions.

Why Christianity? Because it offers us a God who is "Love." We have heard this phrase so often that it has been worn smooth. For most of the world, however, it comes with the force of a fresh revelation. The power of these words can be understood only when we trace the history of man's religious endeavors and find that most of his efforts have been directed toward placating an angry, vindictive, capricious God!

In Westminster Abbey there is a plaque marking the burial place of David Livingstone, immortal missionary of another generation. He was attacked by wild beasts, buried his wife in the jungle, and died on his knees by his cot in Africa. His body was then carried with honor to Westminster Abbey where he lies with kings and queens. It is said that at his funeral they sang his favorite hymn which has in it this line:

> O God of Bethel, by whose hand
> Thy people still are fed. . . .

Through all the vicissitudes of his life he never doubted but that God's sovereign purpose for him was created out of love. This vibrant note runs through the entire Judaeo-Christian witness from the Twenty-Third Psalm with its assurance that "The Lord Is My Shepherd. . . ." to the book of Revelation with these comforting words: "Behold, the dwelling of God is with men. . . . He will wipe away every tear from their eyes, and death shall be no more, neither shall there be mourning nor crying nor pain any more, for the former things have passed away." (Revelation 21:3-4) The philosopher's question is asked in these terms, "Is the universe friendly?" to which the Christian affirms, "God is love."

Eddie Cantor, who was brought up in the slums of New York City's east side, tells in his autobiography how one summer as a youngster he was scooped off the hot and dirty streets and taken to a summer camp along the cool and refreshing Hudson River. For the first time in his memory he had three good meals every day. One night he got to wondering how he happened to be there, why it wasn't costing anything. Another kid in the tent had the answer. "Because somebody's interested in kids like us." Eddie went to sleep that night murmuring to himself, "Thank you, somebody." And then adds, "That was the closest I ever got to religion in those days." This is what Christianity affirms. Somebody's interested in folks like us. We are not in this world alone. God has expressed himself as love.

In the second place, we believe Christianity is unique in offering us a leader who was and is as "no other man." Our doctrinal statement reminds us that "at the heart of the gospel of salvation is God's self-presentation in Jesus of Nazareth. . . . In his life we see the power and wisdom of God, confirming his new covenant with his people in the revelation of the fullness of human possibilities." What is Christian? Is a man a Christian simply by virtue of not being a Muslim or a Buddhist or a Jew? If so, a criminal might justifiably wear the Christian label. Is he a Christian simply because he lives according to the Golden Rule? Any decent and respectable agnostic may fulfill that condition.

To find an answer we must go back to the beginning and remember that when Jesus walked beside the Sea of Galilee there was not another Christian in the world. Peter, Andrew, James, and John were good men who feared God and kept the law, but they could not properly be called Christians. These four fishermen became Christians only on a day when Jesus said, "Follow me," and they forsook their nets and followed him. So we have our answer. A Christian is someone who responds to the call of Christ. First and always, Christianity is a relationship to a Person. In that sense it differs from the world religions like Judaism and Hinduism and all rival faiths that compete for men's allegiance. All these direct our loyalty to a theological system, a code of ethics, a philosophy, or an ideology, but Christianity alone directs our loyalty to a Person. Where Christ is, there is Christianity, and the Christian is a person who tries to be a follower of Jesus Christ.

A leader sets an example. The attack on Pearl Harbor was led by a Captain Fuchida. Later in the war, when General Doolittle carried out his famous raid on Tokyo, one of the American men shot down was a Sergeant Jacob De Shazer. He spent the rest of the war in a Japanese prison camp and received brutal treatment. After the war, he returned to the states, entered seminary, and prepared himself to go as a missionary to Japan. There he and Captain Fuchida met. The Captain was puzzled as to why anyone would come back to Japan after what the Sergeant had gone through.

Then he met a young missionary woman, daughter of two missionaries who had been beheaded by the Japanese during the war. He found all this unbelievable. Why would these people want to spend their lives with their enemies? He secured a copy of the Bible to see what it was all about. When he came to that passage where Jesus, hanging on the cross, prays for his enemies saying, "Father, forgive them, they know not what they do," he understood. Sergeant De Shazer and the young woman were doing what their leader had done.

Christ gave us an example, not only of how to accept hardship, but of how to live with enthusiasm and joy. The New Testament contains enough tragedy to make it the saddest book in the world, but it opens with the songs of angels bringing tidings of great joy, and it closes with the Hallelujah Chorus sung by all the ransomed hosts of heaven.

A young English clergyman, shortly after his ordination, crossed the channel and visited Paris. When he returned, one of his friends asked if he had enjoyed Paris and he said, "Yes, but I wish I had visited it before I was converted." This is representative of what most people believe about religion. It is a negative, something which inhibits and represses. It takes the "fun out of living." We assert that there is not a single thing in this whole world to which you are not entitled if it will do you good and be profitable. Christianity is against drunkenness, because it is destructive. Christianity is against adultery, because it is a sickness. Christianity is against hate and revenge, because they erode your spiritual potential. But everything that is life-fulfilling is yours to enjoy. Jesus lived life from a great depth of being and with joy! And we are to live this way.

Not only does a leader give an example to his followers but he also believes in them and their potential for greatness. We are grateful for the Christian estimate of man as a being of infinite value and worth. The Christian doctrine of man conceives him as bearing the image of God, as an agent of moral discernment, as capable of making a faith response, and as having a personal responsibility for helping establish social structures of equity. Buddhism does not provide this understanding of man, and thoughtful Japanese leaders have expressed a concern as to how long democracy can prevail without a concept of man as a person of unique and inherent dignity. Certainly the Hindu principle of Nirvana (which is final and total escape) cannot provide the impulse for transforming society. In Buddhism it is not transformation of reality but salvation from reality which is the basic attitude. In any religious decalogue the basic question relates to the intrinsic aim of existence. Christianity emphasizes not only the fact of God but also brings man into focus as responsible for the Fall, as a sinner, but who is also capable of a faith response which results in a life committed to establishing the kingdom of God as the ultimate reality.

Christianity is not passive. It believes man can do something about helping to fashion this unfinished creation. It believes man can responsibly involve himself. We are right in the mainstream of Christian affirmation when we sing:

Rise up, O men of God! Have done with lesser things;
Give heart and mind and soul and strength To serve the
  King of Kings.
Rise up, O men of God! His kingdom tarries long;
Bring in the day of brotherhood And end the night of
  wrong.

Christianity also has a uniqueness in that it lays upon us the call to perfection. It recognizes our weakness, but does not temper its claims and demands by our frailty. Again and again, in the Sermon on the Mount, Jesus lays upon his followers the burden of seemingly impossible moral and ethical ideals. Who can really love his enemy? Who can honestly pray for those who despitefully use him? Who can go on and on forgiving in the face of ingratitude? Who can ever measure up to the demand that Jesus phrased in the words, "Be ye therefore perfect, even as your father which is in heaven is perfect"?

The only way to spiritual growth is to reach for that which is always beyond our grasp. We must not become satisfied and fashion ideals to meet our accomplishments. The church must never be a reflection of the morals and ideals of its members. Not a one of us but what feels there is more love to express, more truth to comprehend, more work to be accomplished. Christianity believes man can grow all his life.

Some years ago there was a film about Red Nichols and his Five Pennies. This was the day of the big bands, and the Five

Pennies included Glenn Miller, the Dorsey Brothers and Artie
Shaw. The joy of Red's life was his daughter. She was stricken
with polio. He traveled across a continent to be at her bedside.
Much of the film was devoted to showing how he worked
with his daughter. He always kept pushing her beyond her
grasp. When he brought a puppy home, he would place it
on the hillside and let her climb and stretch and strain for
it. Sometimes it seemed cruel to ask the impossible but it was
the only way she could regain the use of her legs. Growth
is possible only as we strain and stretch, never arriving, never
completely grasping, but always reaching for more knowledge,
more understanding, more love, more of the mind of Christ.

The worth of an ideal is never measured merely by the degree
to which we attain but by the direction it gives life. The flower,
reaching for the sun, never reaches its goal except in responding
to the upward pull; the dynamic of life and growth is within
the flower. We may never in this lifetime attain all that is
implied in the ideal, "Be ye perfect, even as your Father in
heaven is perfect," but in reaching toward that we have within
us the dynamic of growth. We are grateful for a religion and
a faith that keeps expecting great things of us, that keeps us
reaching and growing all of life. Paul said he did not count
himself as having attained, but he was pressing toward the
mark.

There is one final thought. This principle of growth applies
not only to this life but to the world to come. For the problem
of sin and evil, there is the promise of forgiveness, salvation,
and "eternal life." For the problem of suffering, there is the
promise of increasing victory and the final weaving into a joyous
pattern although we may not fully understand until we have
the perspective of eternity. For the problem of death, there
is the promise of survival and reunion. We "lift our eyes above
the shadows of earth and see the light of eternity."

4
HOLY SPIRIT

In the section on "Distinctive Emphases of United Methodists" in the Doctrinal Statement of the 1972 General Conference is this sentence: "One of the most familiar accents in traditional United Methodist teaching has been on the primacy of grace. By grace we mean God's loving action in human existence through the ever present agency of the Holy Spirit." While this is a distinctive emphases, we United Methodists share with all Christians in believing in the Holy Spirit. At times we have neglected this doctrine and we must acknowledge that we have often misunderstood it. But as Bishop Mack Stokes reminds us, "We have been true to New Testament Christianity whenever we stressed the power and presence of the Holy Spirit."

Having affirmed that as United Methodists we believe in the Holy Spirit, we hasten to add that the Christian faith, contrary to what is often assumed, does not have three distinct persons, separate from each other, as God.

The late Cardinal Cushing told in an address to a group of Protestant clergy that when he was a parish priest he was summoned to a store to give the last rites to a man who had collapsed. Following the custom of his church, he knelt by the man and asked: "Do you believe in God the Father, God the Son, and God the Holy Spirit?" He said the man roused a little, opened one eye, looked at the people standing around, and said: "Here I am dying, and he asks me a riddle."

No doctrine is more misunderstood than the Christian concept of the Trinity. When we say "God in three persons, blessed Trinity," however, we are using the word "persons" in the sense in which the word "Persona" was used in the theater of classical Greece and Rome. It meant the mask, put on by actors, in order to play different parts. The word was taken over by early theologians to express the diverse forms of God's activity without destroying the concept of God's unity.

When we use the name, Holy Spirit, we are saying that we believe God can indwell men, inspire men, energize, and motivate them. We are saying that we believe God expresses himself in beauty, truth, goodness, and love. We also believe that the Holy Spirit, as someone has phrased it, "is the unseen Presence rebuking us for every evil thought and deed, confirming us in every good thing, and summoning us to creative advances with God and man." The Doctrinal Statement reminds us that Grace (God's loving action in human existence through the everpresent agency of the Holy Spirit) is the spiritual climate and environment surrounding all human life at all times and in all places. "Prevenient grace" is the divine love that anticipates all our conscious impulses and that persuades the heart toward faith.

When we say, Holy Spirit, we are thinking of the spiritual presence of Jesus of Galilee. Jesus promised, "I will not leave you desolate." And Paul wrote, "If any man have *not* the Spirit of Christ, he is none of his." Furthermore, when the Holy Spirit was poured out upon the disciples at Pentecost, they were convinced that Jesus was back in their midst as he had promised. The presence they experienced was not something strange but the reality of Christ in their midst once again.

The number three is incidental. We are simply saying that these are the ways we know God and we are also saying that all these expressions are manifestations of the One God. We are *mono*-theistic, not *tri*-theistic. When we say, "God the Father, God the Son, and God the Holy Spirit," we are saying that we know God as Sovereign Creator; we know him as revealed in Jesus of Galilee; we know him as a Presence within us now for comfort and for strength.

If this still seems confused, and if the Holy Spirit seems elusive of definition, let's remember that since the personality of man baffles the wisest psychologists of our day, man can hardly hope to do more than make guesses about the supra-personality of a Sovereign God.

It is appropriate, however, that we discover again this distinctive emphasis of our heritage. Both the religious and the secular press carry periodic reports of a surging new spirit of religious fervor sweeping across the land. The major secular magazines have carried articles about the appearance of the glossolalia movement in the old-line churches, including the Roman Catholic. Glossolalia is a term transliterated from the Greek word for "tongue" or "language." The term refers mainly to the so-called "gifts," in 1 Corinthians 12:4. This is the incoherent speech of religious ecstasy. There are many who consider this a sign the believer is possessed of the Holy Spirit. We should remember, however, that this phenomenon caused disorder in the Christian assembly at Corinth. Paul did not outright reject it, but he discussed the problems caused by this "gift" and advocated the principle that all must be done for edification. Since speaking in "tongues" does not conform to this principle, Paul placed prophecy above glossolalia in his list of "gifts of the Spirit."

In general, United Methodists acknowledge the right of an individual to express his devotional feelings in private in the ecstasy of "tongues" but have resisted the public manifestation.

There are too many dangers associated with the movement to make it a central part of our emphasis or tradition. Here and there an individual may resort to glossolalia in his private devotions, but it has rarely been a part of the public worship service in United Methodism.

This does not mean, in the first place, that we are uninterested in the manifestation of the Holy Spirit in our personal and corporate lives. But the results we seek are more functional. Our Doctrinal Statement affirms that the Holy Spirit is the active cause of our justification, by which we are made new creatures in Christ. It is the agency of nurture by which the believers "grow in grace" and in Christian understanding. It is the instrument by which the Christian life is crowned with the perfection of love (sanctification). In this context, the New Testament exhortation that we be filled with the Holy Spirit has found a wide reception and the experience of Pentecost has been restored to its position as normative Christianity. For us, however, normative is not "speaking in tongues" but opening the life to the Holy Spirit in such a way that he can signify God's acceptance and pardoning love, make us new creatures in Christ, perfect us in God's *agape* love, and thereby empower us for effective Christian witness. The baptism with the Spirit is a baptism of love and an empowerment for evangelism or witness.

Wesleyans have generally placed heavy stress on the ethical manifestations of the Spirit's presence. The New Testament sums up the doctrine in this phrase "the spirit of Christ." To John the Baptist, God said, "Upon whom thou shalt see the Spirit descending and remaining on him, the same is he which baptizeth with the Holy Ghost." (John 1:33) At his baptism Jesus was revealed as the Bearer of the Spirit. The descending dove marked him as the Anointed of God. Pentecost disclosed Jesus as the Spirit-Baptizer. In this event the Spirit of God became the Holy Spirit of our Lord Jesus Christ. He became the supreme manifestation, as the Spirit became the medium through whom Christ comes to indwell and sanctify his Church. In other words, Christ is the pattern of the Spirit-filled life. The Holy Spirit is therefore the Christ-Spirit. It was not, however, until Jesus gave up his life forgivingly on the cross that that pattern was complete. "Christ also suffered for us, leaving us an example, that ye should follow his steps . . . who, when he was reviled, reviled not again; when he suffered, he threatened not; but committed himself to him that judgeth righteously." (1 Peter 2:21-23) The Spirit of Jesus is the "Spirit of the Cross." The spirituality recognized in the New Testament has an ethical dimension. When we have "The Spirit," we are Christlike in our suffering, forgiveness, compassion, and caring.

Thus the Christian experience of the Holy Spirit means, primarily, to have "Christ formed in us." When this happens we can say, "For me to live is Christ." Paul prays for God's people who are now the "habitation of God through the Spirit" that "Christ may dwell in (their) hearts by faith." One translation renders this, "That Christ may make his home in your hearts." This is the same as being "filled with all the fulness of God."

It was the spiritual genius of John Wesley that he saw that this sanctification (or perfection of love as the Doctrinal Statement defines it) lies at the very heart of Christ's redemptive activity. One of Wesley's earliest Oxford sermons notes that "the title Holy applied to the Spirit of God does not only denote that he is holy in his own nature, but that he makes us so; that he is the great fountain of holiness to his Church. The Holy Spirit is the principle of the conversion and entire sanctification of our lives." One scholar observes that "Wesleyan theology was preeminently a doctrine of the Holy Spirit." He was bearing witness to the New Testament truth that the Spirit of Christ is the sanctifying Spirit and that all his ministrations are to the end of making us holy and Christlike persons.

Christian perfection was a life of such intimate communion with God, made possible through the sanctifying presence of the Holy Spirit, that the natural fruit of that relationship had ethical dimensions. "We were made perfect in love." The gifts of the Spirit are not "spiritual things" for personal aggrandizement. They are "grace gifts" which make us loving and humble like Jesus. They are those spiritual endowments which enable us to contribute to the common good of the body of Christ. There are those who question whether a gift can be said to "exist" for the individual if it is not employed for the sake of building up the body of Christ in loving unity.

Paul comes to the heights of New Testament truth when he pens, "Now I will show you the best way of all, without which all other gifts are nothing." 1 Corinthians 13 is the way of *agape* love (love given in response to God's love for man, a response in which man gives of himself in building up life). In *A Plain Account of Christian Perfection,* Wesley makes Paul's point clear: "Another ground of a thousand mistakes is, not considering deeply, that love is the highest gift of God; humble, gentle, patient love; that all visions, revelations, manifestations whatever, are little things compared to love; and that all gifts are either the same with, or infinitely inferior to it."

We feel it is important to establish the fact that the gift of the Holy Spirit, bringing sanctification, has a practical and ethical result. We are made "perfect in love." There are, however, other dimensions. The Doctrinal Statement would remind us that "out of our heritage we gratefully reaffirm belief in 'Prevenient grace,' the divine love that anticipates all our conscious impulses and that persuades the heart toward faith. . . . He continues to nurture the believers as they 'grow in grace' and in Christian understanding." Another way of saying this is found in one of the creeds printed in the United Methodist Hymnal which says the Holy Spirit is "God present with us for guidance, comfort, and strength."

The first Christians, left desolate by Jesus' death, found, to their immense joy and faith, that they were not comfortless. They had the experience of Pentecost. They experienced a Presence which continued to comfort, sustain, inspire, and lead. Jesus had told his disciples that he was going away. They felt lonely, fearful, and confused. Then he promised to send another Comforter. "And I will pray the Father, and he shall give you another Comforter, that he may abide with you forever." (John 14:16) The Greek word translated "Comforter" is "paraclete." It literally means "one called to one's side." The Holy Spirit takes the God who is above us and brings him to our side; he transposes the Jesus of history and makes him our living contemporary. The God who is above us has come to us and walks by us, dwells in us, in the person of the Holy Spirit. The hymn writer says:

> Holy Spirit, faithful guide
> Ever near the Christian's side
> Gently lead us by the hand,
> Pilgrims in a desert land.

This comfort comes through prayerful waiting. We are often under such pressure we don't give the Spirit a chance to work in us or come to us. Jesus said, "My peace I leave with you . . . my peace give I unto you." Repentance is also necessary as a prelude to receiving the Holy Spirit as Comforter. The Spirit working in us is the "active cause of our justification, by which we are made new creatures in Christ." Before this can happen, we must repent. Peter was preaching and his listeners were cut to the quick. They cried, "What must we do?" Peter answered, "Repent and be baptized in the name of Jesus Christ, so that you may have your sins forgiven and receive the gift of the Holy Spirit."

The Holy Spirit is the agent of power in the Christian's life. The instruction of Jesus to the disciples was to tarry until endued with power. Life is easily lost in triviality, meaninglessness and frustration. Human experience has demonstrated, however, that when we are touched and quickened by the Holy Spirit, we become valiant and can serve God as we could not do before. The memory of Pentecost haunts us as we recall the power surging in the hearts of the disciples. Where is that power today? Can it come among us again? Undoubtedly we would wish to experience it in an altogether different and new way. We might not look for a dove or tongues of fire. The power we seek must accord with a realistic view of the world. It is the power to care about ourselves and one another and the world. Jesus did not come just to start a new branch of organized religion. His purpose was to redeem mankind, and it was with this purpose that the disciples were so vitally energized at Pentecost. We live in a revolutionary age, full of unrest among students, the blacks, the poor. Jesus was a revolutionary. He talked about faith moving mountains. The Holy Spirit is the source of power for the Christian to get on with the task to which we have been commissioned and to use our personal and social resources in God's way! We must take this doctrine of the Holy Spirit seriously. Not because it will restore the church (though that may happen as a by-product) but because only by becoming bearers of God's redeeming grace can we ourselves hope to be redeemed.

A further function of the Holy Spirit is to give guidance. The Bible is filled with illustrations: In the Old Testament God often made his will known through dreams, visions, and direct conversation. The Gospels tell us that Jesus was led of the Spirit, into the wilderness, back to Nazareth, and through his ministry. In Acts 16:6-10 we are told how the Apostle Paul was led by the Spirit to go to Macedonia and thus the gospel was brought to Europe for the first time. And in the first verse of the Book of Acts there is an interesting idea: Luke writes, "In the first book (the Gospel) I have dealt with all that Jesus began to do and teach. . . ." He began, but didn't finish. In fact, he told his disciples that when he had gone from them the Spirit would come and lead them into all truth. In other words, the Bible is not a closed book. God kept on talking when the book had gone to press. God is a living God and there is truth and guidance for every follower. We are impressed by how many Christian people testify to the idea that they receive divine guidance and leadership when they seek it!

Even as we affirm the reality of divine guidance we must test the spirit! You may feel you have received guidance but we are not infallible. A woman said the Lord told her to leave her husband, but when the husband was consulted he said no such message had been given to him. John Wesley sometimes would let the Bible fall open and then would seize whatever verse his eye found as God speaking to him. I have also done this, but I accompany it with a prayer saying, "Lord, I need help; lead me to a biblical passage that speaks to my need." And it frequently happens. But often it does not. There is the old story of the man seeking help who opened the Bible and the verse he discovered was, "And Judas went and hanged himself." He didn't like that so he tried again and this time the verse was, "Go thou and do likewise."

There are few decisions that are irremediable when a mistake has been discovered. All does not hang on a single judgment. A man who really believes in God counts on the new initiative in life which God with men can always effect, thus he can approach things with a kind of "holy carelessness."

We need also to recognize our capacity for self-deception. We can easily deceive ourselves into thinking that what we want to do is right. (What may seem to be the Holy Spirit may be the devil of self-assertion.) A prison chaplain writes of a study in which he talked with twelve inmates in the penitentiary. He asked each, "Why are you here?" The answers were instructive: "I was framed." "They ganged up on me." "It was a case of mistaken identity." "The police had it in for me." Not one said he was guilty of something. They were all innocent. An insurance adjuster said that he would estimate 90 percent of the people involved in automobile accidents see themselves as blameless.

There are several ways by which the Holy Spirit guides us. Prayer is one but this requires a spirit of genuine. unconditional obedience. Are we willing to take the answer we receive? If not, then we must not expect guidance. Don't expect answers to be dictated, but find a place where you can be quiet, unhurried, and wait. What we should do in prayer is think over the matter carefully in the presence of God, then pray for his guidance and light, asking that he call our attention to facts we may have overlooked. A good prayer is, "Almighty God, our Heavenly Father, unto whom all hearts are open, all desires known, and from whom no secrets are hid, cleanse the thoughts of our hearts by the inspiration of thy Holy Spirit, that we may perfectly love thee, and worthily magnify thy holy name, through Jesus Christ our Lord. Amen."

Through the centuries men have found that the Bible is a lamp unto our feet. Read quickly and then go back and read slowly. Write down any message you feel you have received and then test it. Henry Sloan Coffin, for many years at Union Theological Seminary, tells of two Christian women visiting a family friend in prison. He was unresponsive so they left a Bible. Only after the man's execution did they find a note in which he told how he began reading about Jesus before Pilate, his prayer for his enemies, and then this man said, "I felt a stab at my heart. I don't know what I felt but I know I did believe." The Bible is quicker than a two-edged sword. It is a revealer of truth.

The Holy Spirit guides through the inner voice. We sometimes dull this conscience. Every year the Federal Government receives a rather large sum of money which they call "conscience money." We may smother this inner voice for years, but usually, sooner or later, it breaks through to haunt us. The inner voice has not only the negative value of checking us when we are inclined toward evil, but it also can be an inner guide toward truth and victory. The Bible speaks of "spirit with spirit can meet." God's Spirit and our human spirit can have joyous concourse.

5
BIBLE

Since there is no creed to which all United Methodists must yield allegiance, then by what methods can our doctrinal reflection and construction be most fruitful and fulfilling? This is a question raised by the Doctrinal Statement. The answer comes in terms of our free inquiry within the boundaries defined by four main sources and guidelines for Christian theology: Scripture, tradition, experience, and reason. They provide a broad and stable context for reflection and formulation. They instruct us as we carry forward our never-ending tasks of theologizing.

If Scripture is one of the guidelines for theologizing, for working out our beliefs, what are some of the understandings we bring to the Bible as United Methodists? We believe that while it is only one of the guidelines, it is nevertheless, the primary source for doctrine. We never forget that Christian doctrine has been formed, consciously and unconsciously, from metaphors and themes the origins of which are biblical. "The Bible is the deposit of a unique testimony to God's self-disclosures: in the world's creation, redemption and final fulfillment; in Jesus Christ as the incarnation of God's Word; in the Holy Spirit's constant activity in the dramas of history.

It is the primitive source of the memories, images and hopes by which the Christian community came into existence and that still confirm and nourish its faith and understanding." This statement, coming from the work of the Theological Commission, reveals much of our official stance on the matter of Scripture. We are not literalists; we do not hold to the old notion that it is without error in matters of history and scientific suggestion. We do believe that as we open our minds and hearts to the Word of God through the words of persons inspired by the Holy Spirit, faith is born and nourished, and "both the core of faith and the range of our theological opinions are expanded and enriched."

We do not believe in the method of "proof-texting," that is, finding a passage and then lifting it out of its context in support of some particular idea. We do affirm Scripture texts "are rightly interpreted in the light of their place in the Bible as a whole, and this is illumined by scholarly inquiry and personal insight." It is obvious that the meaning of each text is best understood when its original intention and significance have been grasped. We also believe that there is a practical relevance to the study of Scripture. When it is carefully handled, under the guidance of the Holy Spirit, "we may apply the truth to the circumstances of our time and place."

With these ideas from our Doctrinal Statement in the Book of Discipline as background, let us now examine in some detail what this means for us. First, the Bible is the source of the "memories, images, and hopes by which the Christian community came into existence. . . ." All this was dramatized and brought to focus when the Third Assembly of the World Council of Churches developed and enlarged the definition of the World Council. The definition originally was this: "It is a fellowship of churches which accept our Lord Jesus Christ as God and Saviour." Succinct and simple—there it was. Now two things happened to bring about an enlargement of the definition. The first was the inclusion of the Russian Orthodox Church which brought a conviction that there should be a reference to the Holy Trinity. The second was a feeling on the part of many protestant churches that there should be some reference made to Scripture. Combining these two emphases, the definition was enlarged to read: "The World Council of Churches is a fellowship of churches which confess the Lord Jesus Christ as God and Saviour according to the Holy Scripture, and therefore seek to fulfill their common calling to the glory of one God, Father, Son, and Holy Spirit." Through this procla-mation of the new definition, we have brought into focus the relevance of the Scriptures for the Christian tradition.

A second thought relates to inspiration. The theory of verbal inspiration of the Bible holds that the human author was simply a mouthpiece of God; God dictated the Bible, so that every word represents the divine mind. This mechanical theory of inspiration is rejected by most United Methodist scholars who view the Scriptures as historically conditioned although they do believe the Holy Spirit was acting upon the human agent. One way of suggesting this idea is the approach taken by Luther. He said that God is in every syllable, but Luther still recognized errors and inconsistencies in the Scriptures. For example, he saw the differences between the birth stories in Matthew and Luke. He also recognized that some books were of more value than others. He said the Epistle of James is an epistle of straw. In other words, the principle of inspiration was accepted, uniformity of inspiration was not. Inspiration does not mean verbal dictation. Most scholars conclude that it is the truths which are inspired and not the words, which are merely the vehicles of truth. It is important to distinguish between word-pictures and the truth they are intended to convey.

How should we, with all our knowledge of physics, biology, and geology, of anthropology, paleontology, and astronomy, understand such biblical stories as the creation of man, the stories of devils and demons, of speaking animals? Are not these stories a flagrant contradiction of what modern science and technology tell us?

Rudolph Bultmann, who stirred considerable controversy with his essay "The New Testament and Mythology," stressed that we are to take these stories seriously. But they require interpretation. He calls this process demythologizing. The biblical message has come to us in the language and thought patterns of the people whom God moved to write it.

That ancient world view, Bultmann says, is "mythological" over against the rational-scientific world view of our time with its different emphasis on cause-and-effect relationships. We must, therefore, interpret the biblical message in the categories in which modern man tends to think.

There are over eleven hundred known human languages. A translator must use extreme ingenuity to convey sense and truth where word-for-word transmission is out of the question. You cannot talk to tribes who live without ever seeing navigable water of our possessing "an anchor of the soul." You cannot speak to the Eskimos of "the lamb of God" or of Christ being "the true vine."

Paul was struggling with human words to express something of the wonders which, he senses, lie beyond observable life. When he spoke of Christ ascending "up on high" he was not really talking of some location a certain number of miles above the earth's surface. We talk of high ideals or of a high purpose or of a failing business as going downhill. In similar fashion Paul used expressions of height and depth as useful symbols but not as geographical locations. The New Testament uses picture language. But we do that. The accountant speaks of frozen assets, and the town-planner refers to a "bottleneck." There is, however, a real situation behind each of the shorthand pictures and there is a reality behind every Christian expression.

Because picture language is sometimes used, it does not follow that the actual events are unhistorical or mythical.

At one time the Roman Catholic catechism had this question: "Who founded the Roman Catholic Church?" and the answer given was, "Jesus Christ." The next question read, "Who founded other denominations and churches?" and the answer was, "Ordinary men like you and me." In this ecumenical age this set of questions is rarely used. But the appropriate answer could be "both."

We believe the Bible is a result of the efforts of both the Holy Spirit and ordinary men. Furthermore, all churches were founded by ordinary men even as they strive to embody the teaching and the spirit of Jesus Christ. The work of ordinary men can be seen as we trace the contribution of men in bringing the Bible down the ages to us. Review for a moment where we got the Bible.

Not one single word of the original writings remains. The ancient Hebrew people had sacred writings. We do have fragmentary records dating back to about 650 B.C. These writings were referred to as "The Law," "The Prophets," "Other Sacred Writings." All were written in ancient Hebrew characters.

About 200 B.C. a group of "learned fathers," seventy in all, gathered in Alexandria, Egypt and carefully collected and translated their Sacred Writings into Greek, primarily for the use of the Jews in that area. But the Jews in Egypt and the Jews in Palestine could not agree upon what constituted the "Holy Writings" as there were many other similar writings claiming authenticity. The Alexandrians wished to include many of the Apocryphal Books while the Palestinian Jews stood for the list of Books as we have them in our Authorized Version. The latter, the Old Testament as we have it, without the Apocrypha which is in the Catholic Bible, is the Scriptures which Jesus knew and from which he quoted.

During the latter part of the First Century A.D. the New Testament books were completed. They came from many sources and there is no common theme through them all. They were written in Aramaic and Greek. They were widely distributed, read, passed to others. Athanasius, bishop of Alexandria, promulgated a canonical New Testament list in his Easter letter of A.D. 367. This list is famous as the first to include just the books found in our New Testament today.

The first great translation of the Bible into a living language was the "Vulgate" in Latin, completed by Jerome in Bethlehem, about A.D. 400. Revised and retranslated by a Church Council it remains as the Douay Version which has been the official Bible of the Roman Catholic Church.

Wycliffe completed the first translation of the Bible into English or Saxon in 1382. It was handwritten and so highly prized that there is the record of one eager Christian who gave a load of hay in order that he might have a day with a copy of the Scripture. Tyndale finished the first real translation into the common language of the people. This was published in 1525 and was one of the first books printed. He was martyred for his effort because there was considerable opposition to putting the Scripture in the language of the people. Church authorities feared that if it were available to the people they would misinterpret its meaning and corrupt its influence. Then in 1611 there was the Authorized Version which we familiarly call the King James Version. This was a scholarly and consecrated attempt to revise, correct, and harmonize all previous translations. The beauty, grandeur, and magnificence of this translation have never been surpassed.

The influence of Scripture on western civilization cannot be overemphasized. Our conversation is liberally sprinkled with phrases out of the Scripture. We speak of "the salt of the earth," "apple of the eye," "skin of the teeth," "filthy lucre," "labor of love," and "beating our spears into plow shares." All these phrases are lifted directly out of the Scripture.

It was the judgment of H. G. Wells that "the Bible has been the Book that held together the fabric of western civilization. It has been the handbook of life to countless millions of men and women. The civilization we possess could not have come into existence and could not have been sustained without it."

In all this we are simply trying to say that the Bible is a very human book in its origins and translations, and has profoundly influenced our human institutions in western civilization. But it also contains the inspired Word of God. Buried under the ancient figures of speech which it uses to express its ideas, the careful and serious reader finds within the Bible eternal truths which will serve to guide him in his search for the meaning of life. It will be necessary to improve our mechanical equipment and redesign our scientific instruments, but we will never find it necessary to amend the great moral and spiritual principles which it sets forth.

For years J. B. Phillips, noted scholar in Great Britain, looked upon the Scriptures with something akin to disdain. He was a linguist and after spending years with classical Greek he considered New Testament Greek in about the same category as a Shakespearean scholar would consider the weekly letter from the pastor to the congregation. During World War II he remembered Paul's letters were written to those in danger. "As I began translating these epistles," he later wrote, "my conviction grew that the New Testament was in a quite special sense inspired. It is not magical; nor is it faultless. Human beings wrote it. But by something which I would not hesitate to describe as a miracle there is a concentration upon that area of inner truth which is fundamental and ageless. That, I believe, is the reason why millions of people have heard the voice of God speaking to them through these seemingly artless pages."

A third question is that of authority. Medieval thinking was dominated by the idea of authority. This was generally assumed to be derived from the tradition of the elders and the dicta of the Church as the depository, guardian, and interpreter of that tradition. The historic continuity of the faith was the major emphasis when talking about authority. Thinking was rigidly controlled, and nothing that we now know as freedom and scholarship was tolerated or even conceivable. The argument that tradition was more important than Scripture rested on the assertion that the Church existed before the Bible. Authority for the Roman Catholic derived from the Church, which was headed by the living representative of Christ, the Pope. The Church was the depository of "the truth delivered by our elders" and private judgment in the interpretation of Scriptures was denied.

The Reformation was a break with this attitude. The Reformers maintained that the authority for the doctrines which they held rested on Scripture. In other words, the basis for authority in the Reformation church was shifted from the Church, headed by the Pope, to the "Scriptural precedent and primitive example." This point of view generally still prevails in Protestantism and is illustrated by the fact that when new members are received into The United Methodist Church the question is asked: "Do you receive and profess the Christian faith as contained in the Scriptures of the Old and New Testaments?" The faith found in the Scripture is what binds us. There is no hierarchial structure within United Methodism that has authority over the individual in spiritual matters. The General Conference may speak for us in issues that pertain to polity and structure, but in the matters of the faith it can only speak to us of emphases and offer guidelines. The source of authority for the individual is in Scripture.

This is an age, however, that raises questions, not only about the authority of the Bible, but about the value of all authority. What is the point of teaching or studying the classical disciplines, including the Bible, when the bases for our action are given with sufficient clarity by contemporary ethics and the adjunct studies of sociology and psychology? I suspect many of us, if our back were against the wall, would honestly have to answer, "Very little indeed." There is probably a widespread, intuitive acceptance of two affirmations: (1) The New Testament and the creeds are no longer in any way authoritative or canonical for us; (2) The Christian today can find sufficient guidelines for his faith and action in contemporary statements and solutions.

Without disrespect, we can admit that the Bible does not have scientific authority in the material realm. Christianity was originally propagated in an age ignorant of the scientific facts that began to come to light with the Copernican revolution in cosmology. But let's not worry too much about that. Even the astronauts made reference to "sunset" and of all people they knew that was not a scientific truth but they did not let technical knowledge rob them of the spiritual insights that are a valid witness to truth.

Remember this, the Bible does have the authority of valid human experience. Experience is costly and sometimes painful. Unfortunately, as a proverb reminds us, experience is like giving an expensive comb to a man who has lost his hair. You have learned from the experience, but now it's too late. Reading the Scripture is a way of learning from the experiences of others. We do not observe the Ten Commandments because they are in the Scripture. If this were the only reason for observing them, most of us would not heed their counsel. We feel that the Ten Commandments are true because they are the summation, they are the crystalization of the experiences of earlier generations. They say to us, "If you want to know how to live creatively, meaningfully, then here are guides that will help you."

It also has the authority of spiritual truth. Consider its insights. You feel you have done your best. What next? Paul tells the Ephesians in four words what it is, "Having done all, stand." Relax, stand quietly, quit trying to overcome with just your conscious mind. "Underneath are the everlasting arms." One of the deepest forms of communication is touch. We are born with the fear of falling. The idea of being sustained with loving arms speaks to our need for security. "Love thy neighbor as thyself." Lack of self-esteem is the most common emotional ailment. Read the story of the Prodigal Son. How can we feel permanently rejected or condemned with this magnificent promise: "Take no thought for the morrow!" A modern rephrasing might be, "Stop worrying about the future." "Sufficient unto the day are the evils thereof." We have problems right now. "They that wait upon the Lord shall mount up with wings of eagles." "Where your treasure is, there will your heart be also." We know the validity of this. What is important to you? "You will know the truth and the truth will make you free!" The goal of psychotherapy is to bring us to that place where we have the strength to face the truth about ourselves. Spiritual truth is more than cognitive; it is relational, personal, inner, and life-changing. "What is man . . . thou hast crowned him a little lower than the angels." On this affirmation about the dignity of man rests our concept of freedom and democracy. Western civilization has drawn upon the biblical idea of man for its definition of government. The Bible does carry the authority of valid spiritual insights—truths tested by the centuries of human experience.

We are not, however, a Bible reading people. In a certain high-school English class 88 percent of the students could not name the four Gospels. One said that three of them are Christianity, Hinduism, and confusion, but he didn't know the fourth. At the University of Denver, a student was asked on a test, "Tell what you know about Moses." He answered frankly, "All I know about Moses is that he is dead."

Our neglect of the Bible, while unfortunate, is understandable. The occasional Bible reader is overwhelmed by the strangeness of the Bible's content. It is a conglomeration of material on a wide variety of subjects, written on two continents, in three languages, by many different authors scattered over a thousand years. Furthermore, there are so many difficult questions. The Gospel of Luke tells us that Jesus was born of a virgin. Yet the gospel of Matthew traces his genealogy back to David through Joseph. How do you reconcile that? Why do we have four Gospels instead of one, when they tell the same basic story? Why two Old Testament histories—Kings and Chronicles? Who can understand all the imagery of Revelation? How did the erotic passages in Ezekiel and the Song of Solomon ever slip by the censors?

All this, however, should not deter us in our effort to understand and apply the Scripture. The simple fact is that this literary expression of the religious development of the Hebrew people culminating in the life and teachings of Jesus is required reading for those who would call themselves Christian. The Bible is the story of Jesus Christ. He is the unifying principle. He gives meaning to the Old Testament. Our doctrinal statement would remind us that "the Bible is the deposit of a unique testimony to God's self-disclosures . . . in Jesus Christ as the incarnation of God's Word." The procession of laws, genealogies and love songs, of ancient history, priests and prophets, of faith and despair, make sense because it all leads to Christ. This is, for the Christian, the basic reason for studying the Bible. William Warren Smart once said, "There is probably not a person living who could, over a considerable period of time, spend twenty minutes a day in the presence of Jesus as the Gospels have pictured him without having his life profoundly influenced by him one way or another."

When we look at Christ we remember that God has identified himself with our condition. Elie Wiesel, a gifted Israeli journalist, spent years in a concentration camp and was overwhelmed by the evidence of evil in his fellow prisoners and in his surroundings. One day he was forced to watch the hanging of a young boy by the Gestapo, a hanging that lasted more than half an hour because the boy's body was so light. As he strangled to death in indescribable agony, most of his fellow prisoners stood in stunned silence. One man spoke for them all as he cried out repeatedly, "Where is God now? Where is God now?" Deep within his own life, Elie Wiesel was certain of the answer, "God is there on the gallows—dead."

But George McLeod affirmed it this way: "Jesus Christ was not crucified in a cathedral between two candles, but on a cross between two thieves; on the town garbage heap; on a crossroads so cosmopolitan that they had to write his title in Hebrew and Latin and Greek; at the kind of place where cynics talk smut, and thieves curse, and soldiers gamble. Because this is where he died and that is what he died about."

The Bible makes it plain that God is not dead, but involved in all that hurts and destroys the vision and hope of man. The men of the Bible were honest men, making an honest search for God. They struggled with doubt and fear and uncertainty. As the Bible talks about this, no questions are avoided; no issues evaded; no difficulties glossed over. And through it all looms the figure of one who was crucified between two thieves at the crossroads, revealing a God who touches us in the moment of need and struggle.

When we look to the Christ revealed in Scripture, we discover God's call to mission. We know of his mandate. As we look at Christ, we know what God is like and what he expects of us. And the call is to "take up your cross and come follow me."

When we look to the Christ revealed in Scripture, we catch a vision of the hope eternal! At a recent discussion about the church, a young person said, "I don't want to hear any more sermons about heaven! Heaven can wait! I want help now on how to live each day as I face choices about drugs, sex, career, and marriage. I could care less about heaven!" This is an understandable feeling. When you are young the issues of the moment are so urgent. It is our faith that Jesus, who died relatively young, could understand this. In fact, a "rich young ruler" came running to him with a request for additional knowledge about the secrets of life. But there comes a moment when the decisions of drugs, sex, and career are no longer paramount. We yearn for something "beyond." We are ready to go home.

Bible reading can be more meaningful if first, one of the modern translations is used. The King James version was an effort to put the Scripture into the language of its day. The Bible is more understandable if it is read in the idiom of our day. Second, buy a commentary. This will give the background of each book, by whom written, to whom, for what purpose, an outline, and the central idea or theme. With this in mind, the message becomes more easily discernible. Third, keep it available. Many carry a small vest-pocket edition of the New Testament to use when there are a few spare moments available. Daily reading can give a new sense of direction and balance.

It is important to be selective in reading. Don't start with Genesis and read toward Revelation. It is a library, not a book. Start with the Gospel of Mark, for with its sharp reportorial style one can get an insight into the Man of Galilee. Move from that into the story of Acts where the heroism of those who established the missionary church is recorded. Reach into the Old Testament and study some of the fathers of the Faith.

Listen to the music in the style of the Apostle Paul, particularly in First Corinthians. When in a reflective mood try some of the Psalms. If one reads selectively, knowing a little of the background, the message will come alive and speak to your deepest need.

Above all, read it devotionally. Let the Holy Spirit speak to you through the sacred pages. It is not wise to be overly concerned about passages that seem difficult or contain apparent contradictions. Always approach it with the question, "What is God saying to me from these pages of Holy Writ?" Read it to catch the mind and spirit of the heroes of the faith. Read it to discover Christ. And when you do this, you will find a fire and zeal kindling in your own heart that will bring you to the portals of heaven!

6
CHURCH

"The United Methodist view of faith and its fruits is linked with a distinctive emphasis on polity. In our understanding of the church, there has been a long-standing tension between our original image of small, voluntary 'religious societies' organized for Christian fellowship, and the worldwide church which has developed in the course of two centuries. . . . On the one hand, the basic premise of the small group is the principle of 'subsidiarity' or voluntary association and local initiative. It is in the local communities and in small groups within them that the Holy Spirit nurtures meaningful experiences which then seek wider avenues of mission and outreach. On the other hand, United Methodists, believing themselves led by the same Spirit, have a long tradition of connectional administration which binds us together in seeing our task as a whole, in efficient planning, and in deploying our material and human resources."

This statement implies a need for the organized community of believers and suggests the church has two responsibilities. The first is to provide the setting in which the Holy Spirit can nurture meaningful religious experience. The second is to "connect" with other congregations in such a way that there can be the effective deploying of material and human resources.

Let us first examine the question as to the necessity of any organization. A youth delegate to an annual conference said, "We have Jesus; why do we need the church?" We are committed to the idea that even in the midst of a revolutionary time in church history, one that may alter radically the present structuring of congregational life, the established community of believers is still an instrument through which the Holy Spirit may work and few of us are willing to rush out and commit institutional suicide.

When Karl Barth made his lecture tour here in the States not too long before his death, he said: "When theology confronts the Word of God and its witnesses, its place is very concretely in the community, not somewhere in empty space. . . . It is the commonwealth gathered, founded, and ordered by the Word of God, the 'Communion of Saints.' " T. S. Eliot once asked a pertinent question, "What life have you if you have not life together? There is no life that is not in community, and no community not lived in praise of God."

There is still the need for the quietly committed institutional church where people worship, listen to preaching, study in classes, and share in fellowship. For many years the Reverend Jerry Walker was pastor of the old St. James Church on Chicago's South Side. While doing research for Methodism's Bicentennial in Baltimore, he came across an intriguing idea. But let him describe it. "George Whitefield," he said, "was a greater preacher than Francis Asbury but little came from Whitefield's oratory because it was never organized. Asbury was not so eloquent but he left us the Methodist Church." Then Mr. Walker continued, "Side by side in Chicago slums I witnessed secularly-oriented churches become conformed to the world. Community renewal, let alone Christian renewal, did not stem from these. It was the worshipping congregation in that slum area that showed a real sense of spiritual power and which, in the long pull, demonstrated the resources for both personal and community renewal. It was a quietly committed institutional church which was the real guts of hope in a seemingly hopeless situation. Where God was placed above man and love of man was an imperative stemming from love and worship of God, the institution renewed itself and became a growing force in the renewal of the community." It is our conviction as United Methodists that when all the innovations have been tried and all the theories promoted there will still be a need for the people of God to join together in worship, thus equipping themselves for their ministries.

Harvey Cox has reminded us that our generation may be more religious in expression, but less religious in institution. It is true that institutions may become introverted, self-serving, lacking in abrasive, and insensitive to their original missionary impulse. Nevertheless, we still say a word in behalf of some kind of organization for, when the Spirit is present, there is a thrust toward servanthood and community, and this must be coordinated.

Acts 4:32 is a forerunner of the modern commune, for it says that "the company of those who believed were of one heart and soul, and . . . had everything in common." This would require organized cooperation. Chapter six indicates that there was a division of responsibility in the early church as they picked seven men, full of the Spirit, to serve tables. In First Corinthians, the Apostle Paul points out that there are varieties of gifts and varieties of service but the same Spirit. And he makes it quite clear that, when the Spirit comes, there is unity in diversity; there is harmony; and there is organization for the purposes of the divine mission.

The "Religion in America Series" has a book by Charles Ferguson on the Methodists and the making of America. It is titled *Organizing to Beat the Devil*. The author reminds us that the Greeks had a word for it, but the United Methodists have a pamphlet for it. He concludes by saying that our omni-present sense of legal order and parliamentary procedure can be summed up in the apocryphal story of the action of the official board of laymen in a local church who, upon hearing that their pastor was ill, voted thirteen to twelve to pray for him.

Mr. Ferguson tells of Charles McCabe, an Ohio preacher who, in 1862, enlisted in the war against the Confederacy. He was captured and put in a prison for officers in Richmond. Since he possessed the Methodist penchant for organization, he immediately divided his fellow prisoners into classes and by using the various talents in the group, he established the "University of Libby Prison." He is best remembered, however, as a singer who popularized the "Battle Hymn of the Republic." His many talents were acknowledged and rewarded by the church which elected him a Bishop.

On one occasion, he was asked to preside at the General Conference. Soon, there were about a dozen motions on the floor and the parliamentary procedure had degenerated into an uproar. He pounded the gavel and said: "The brethren are getting restless. Let's stand and sing." He broke into the opening lines of "In the Sweet Bye and Bye." The clamor subsided as the delegates began: "There's a land that is fairer than day, and by faith we can see it afar." After the hymn, according to legend, Bishop McCabe said: "By faith we can see the promised land; but we had better get organized if we are going to get there!"

The Spirit brings liberation, but the faith must be nurtured by a community of believers. High resolves need the rein-forcement of the group. When people start looking in the same direction, they are drawn together, and this results in some kind of organization.

We have been saying that organization and "connectionalism" are necessary if we are to have much effectiveness. There must be the instrument by which human and material resources can be deployed. There is also, however, a need for recognizing the concept of "subsidiarity," that is, maintaining the small group concept where the spiritual nature can be nurtured and where men and women can meet God. This is basically why the church exists.

Paul made reference to the prophetic charisma. Peter defended the apostles on the day of Pentecost by saying that they were not drunk, but that God had poured out his Spirit upon them and sons and daughters were prophesying.

Louis Armstrong once said about jazz music: "If I have to explain it to you, then you ain't got it." Perhaps we can't explain all this suggests, but I think it means that the contemporary church must not be afraid of the emotional, the mystical, the subjective, the devotional. For it is this that humanizes life.

A church is not some kind of machine to produce money for headquarters or grind out figures for a statistical column. It is people who dream dreams; who have visions; who get drunk out of frustration; who sweat so their kids can have a chance; who one day love, the next day fight with their marriage partners; who sometimes come to church when they would rather play golf; and who finally die of a coronary or carcinoma. Through it all they are so hungry for a real taste of God that it is often like a sharp pain down deep! Frankly, you should not go to any church unless it offers you an outside chance of a glimpse of God that literally takes away your breath and knocks you to your knees.

In an issue of the "Kiplinger Washington Letter," which is not designed for a young audience, there was this word of instruction for retailers: "Pay more attention to changing fads, styles . . . notice what the youngsters are doing and wearing, what interests them, what TV shows they tune in. Why? To keep your stocks 'hot'. . . . Customers are young and getting younger. But many retailers are middle-aged . . . and may disapprove of youngsters' styles. Bad mistake."

The church must be responsive to the requirements of the one-half of the American population that is under twenty-seven. We must remember their experiences. They have read Kahlil Gibran; in "Superstar" they have listened to Mary Magdalene sing: "I don't know how to love him." They have heard George Harrison talk about, "My Sweet Lord," and Judy Collins proclaim, "Amazing grace, how sweet the sound that saved a wretch like me." They have sought for meaning through such movies as "Alice's Restaurant," and affirmed a readiness to accept the uniqueness of persons in such films as "Easy Rider." They have showed moral courage in going to Washington, several hundred-thousand strong, and in joining with others in singing, "We shall overcome," as they declared to the government with unmistakable clarity that the time had come to stop the nonsense in Vietnam. Their religion, though perhaps not called by that name, has been one of thought, feeling, action, and spontaneity.

Martin Marty, church historian and associate editor of *The Christian Century*, has indicated that the spread of the occult and of Eastern religions is giving Christianity a needed nudge toward its original moorings. He has said: "We have been so busy in Christianity in recent years that we've stopped meditating. Now the fashionable Eastern religions are teaching the younger generation to be still and to know that God is God and to meditate. I do not think that Buddhism is going to replace Christianity, nor that astrology is going to replace Judaism. Rather, there will be a kind of rebirth of a sense of wonder and mystery which are dimensions of our faith we have let drop. . . ."

In an effort to respond to this movement many churches are trying to take a second look at the experiential and emotional developments without falling prey to the excesses of the "grope-and-touch" groups or "body-celebration" traps. They are trying to understand the revival of transcendental impulses and the survival of Pentecostal forms in some of the traditional churches even when put off by some of the less lovable aspects.

What all this means is the suggestion that you seek a church that is not afraid of the dimension of subjective experience. Find a church that understands that it exists for one fundamental reason: to help create conditions in which you may encounter God. Don't worry about the old arguments about pietism versus activism. This is about as silly as arguing about which is more important, to inhale or exhale. Any religion worthy of the name will include both.

The last two decades have brought many changes to the church. During the nineteen-fifties there was the exhilaration of popular acceptance—banners flying—and of numerical growth. In the nineteen-sixties, there was often a sense of ambiguity, of uncertainty, even of embarrassment. Our theological notes were muted and our role lacked precise definition. We felt left out of things by intoxicating but remotely based movements. Now that radical theology has virtually passed and revolutionary calls are somewhat silenced, we, on the local scene, overwhelmed by a sense of realism about the limits of human possibility, nevertheless feel it has fallen to the parish situation to make some small dent on a world of injustice.

A sociologist was recently asked why men enroll in divinity schools. His answer may not speak for you, but this is the way he viewed it. He said:

> Almost nobody goes to win a good name or honor. They enroll because many of them awaken during college to the fact that religion is one of the few approaches to humanizing the world. . . . They despair of other societal institutions and have some hope that religion and its

institutions—weak, frail, and self-serving as they may be—are more malleable to change and provide an opportunity to serve.

There was a fellow who caught a taxi in New York City during a torrential rain. He complained to the driver: "This weather is terrible." To this the driver responded: "It's better than none."

We hold up the local church as a possible arena for service if for no other reason than the one: "It's better than none!" The fact remains that the local church can provide a handle for doing something about our neglected elderly in America. It may not be reaching them, but it is an institution that has access to some three-fourths of our youth. It has a chance to minister to blue-collar, ethnic America. It is right in the middle of the boredom and drama of suburbia.

The church is not only the community of service, but also of love. Jesus, "The Man for Others," sought the support of the twelve, precarious as their companionship proved to be. For millions of our fellow countrymen, loneliness is an ever-present, dull pain. One of the things the church has rediscovered in recent years is that fellowship is intrinsic to the faith rather than being something that is added. Koinonia groups for prayer, witness, and study are again flourishing. The concept of the "Body of Christ," with the members responsible for one another, is once more a living reality.

Recently, a Yokefellow group wrote a paraphrase of Matthew 11:28-30. It reads:

When you feel weighed down by physical, mental, or spiritual burdens, open your heart to my love, because I want very much to help you. Put your hand in mine and let's walk the road of life together. Listen to what I say to you, because what I say will be to help you, not to hurt you. I love you and understand you deeply. I don't expect you to be self-sufficient or equal to every situation, but I am ready to be with you and help you every minute of every day. . . . I only ask you to take the share of the weight you are ready and eager to carry.

If somewhere, somehow, you can discover this kind of vital, Spirit-filled community, rejoice, for indeed, your reward is great. Cherish it as a gift of God. To discover this kind of mutual trust is to taste for yourself the fruit of the Spirit.

Now a final word about our sense of hope for the church. There has been a lot of negative thinking. Notice the headlines. "United Methodist Church loses members." "Church attendance continues to sag!" "General Conference disrupted by protest!" These are the headlines. What do they mean for us who have responsibility within the local church?

It has been quite popular in recent years to refer to this as a "Post-Christian World." Bonhoeffer coined an interesting phrase, "Religionless Christianity." That is, the faith might survive but you would not see any outward expression of it. John Cardinal Wright, key American advisor at the Vatican, recently said: "This is the winter for Christianity. It will continue until something cataclysmic happens. . . ."

Let's look at the positive. First, God will not leave himself without a witness. We may or may not be a part of it, but the witness will be there. Hitler said the church was hollow and he could destroy it in a year, but the church has been an anvil on which a good many hammers have worn out.

Second, the facts may not be as gloomy as we think. A newspaper had an article about church attendance and quoted the Gallup Poll. The headline read, "Catholic churchgoing down: Protestant rate is constant." The percentage in Protestantism has not changed in six years; the Catholics have declined 11 percent.

The World Service dollar is down, but the total giving is at an all time high. Congregations are just less willing to send money to headquarters. They want to spend some of it on projects they can see.

Third, this is not a post-Christian world. Someone, writing about this, says that this would suggest there was a time when the world was Christian. When did this exist? Was it the day of the early church, the day of pagan Rome, the era of the martyrs? Was it the fourth century when Constantine proclaimed Christianity the official religion of the empire and then used it primarily as a tool of conquest, massacre, and slavery?

Was it the Dark Ages, the very adjective description denying the principle that Christ is the light of the world? Could it have been the Middle Ages, when life was crude, boorish, and short?

Would you apply the term "Christian" to the eighteenth and nineteenth centuries, the age of slavery, colonialism, industrial exploitation? And certainly it was not the first half of the twentieth century when the chief condition was war upon war, each one stooping more deeply into savagery and barbarity. So when did the Christian era ever exist?

There is as much opportunity in our age as any. In fact, we may be on the verge of some startling developments. Stephen Neill, in *Call to Mission* predicts that Africa, by the year 2,000 will be the most Christian of the continents. One reason for this is that 80 percent of the literate people in tropical Africa received at least a part of their education in the mission schools. With the demise of the old tribal religions, there is a vacuum into which the Christian faith can move and the African people are acquainted with its truth.

Fourth, it is well to remember, when the doing is difficult, that Christianity was never a majority force. Christians always seem to be a little on the wrong side of history, or a little out of step. But this is precisely the point. It is through a dedicated minority that God's work gets done. The notion of a saving remnant is still valid. Jesus spoke of his disciples as the leaven working in the loaf, as salt giving flavor to the whole. Louis Cassels in a recent column made reference to the fact that the Christian Church, in every generation, is saved by a cadre of dedicated men and women who take the cross. It's never a mass movement! The Reverend R. W. Hugh Jones delivered a presidential address to the annual Assembly of the Congregational Church in England and Wales. Speaking in Westminster Chapel, he said: "We are frightened by falling numbers. Sometimes we are urgently concerned with numbers because we are absorbed by and obsessed with the thought of making the Church successful. The very thought is irrelevant. We are not here to make the Church successful. We are here to burn ourselves out in service for Christ. This is the only valid interpretation of success. But this is not always the image we project. More frequently it is that of men sitting around a table, grey with anxiety wondering how to raise enough money to preach the gospel which tells men not to be anxious."

Fifth, there is a hunger, an openness to a searching for spiritual truth. It is in, for example, the large number of message songs, produced by the media. *The New York Times*, reviewing records, said: "If there is any news in the pop record world today, it is that the influence of the gospel—which Webster defines as the good news concerning Christ—is preempting the influence of almost everything else."

When our Lord said we must become like children, we take it to mean trust, receptivity, and simplicity; but what typifies the child more is his curiosity. With this in mind, the religious outlook is by no means as gloomy as some would have us believe. If we refuse to be sandbagged by statistics of church membership and influence and instead listen to the living voice of this generation, we can't miss the note of awakening religious curiosity. College students may stay away from chapel in droves, but they are demanding courses in religion as never before.

You can find Kierkegaard, Tillich, Kahlil Gibran, Augustine, and the Koran jostling among the textbooks and the pornography on any bookrack.

The contemporary church must regain a sense of victory and purpose, however, if it is to meet the expressed hunger for spiritual reality. Sociologist Peter Berger gave an address at the annual meeting of the Consultation on Church Union. He bluntly told the ecumenists that their efforts to regroup as one big church was a waste of time unless Protestantism regained its self-confidence. He said, "It is time to stop asking what modern man has to say to the church and to turn to the more significant question, 'What does the church have to say to modern man?'" Then Mr. Berger answered his own question. He said: "It's the old story of God's dealings with man spanning the Exodus to Easter morn." The church is custodian of the message for which the world hungers.

7
CONVERSION

Our Doctrinal Statement affirms that "another United Methodist family trait has been an active stress on conversion and a new birth. Whatever our language or labels for it, we hold that a decisive change in the human heart can and does occur under the promptings of grace and the guidance of the Holy Spirit. Such a change may be sudden, dramatic, gradual, cumulative. Always it is a new beginning in a process. Christian experience as personal transformation expresses itself in many different thought-forms and life-styles. All of these have a common feature: faith working by love."

No theme has been more central to United Methodists than the necessity of the "New Birth." Our passion for evangelism grows out of the firm conviction that man must be "born again." We believe there is no substitute for this. John's Gospel reports that early in the ministry of Jesus a Jewish ruler, Nicodemus, visited him to inquire the way to the kingdom of God. Even though he had wealth, status, and a noble heritage, Nicodemus had a spiritual hunger that moved him to seek Jesus. An astute man, he began the conversation by complimenting Jesus, saying that no one could do what he was doing unless God was with him. Jesus responded to this with the abrupt affirmation: "Ye must be born again."

Few passages of Scripture have been more variously interpreted than this imperative: "Be born again," or, "Be born anew." To many it is as bewildering a concept as it was to Nicodemus. The unchurched think of it as vaguely related to revivalist preaching and exhortation. They shrug it aside because they want no part of what they consider to be some kind of emotionalism. Because of such unfortunate association the man on the street and even many within the church have been inclined to disregard the whole concept of conversion as unnecessary or even undesirable.

The best of our theologians, however, and those with spiritual insight have not so regarded it. Edwin Lewis, for many years the distinguished professor of theology at Drew University, has written: "Jesus confronted the astonished Nicodemus . . . (and) told him that the purpose of a man's being born once was that he might be born a second time, and until he was born a second time the purpose of his being born the first time remained unfulfilled. 'That which is born of the flesh is flesh.' This is creaturehood. 'That which is born of the Spirit is spirit.' This is sonship."

God's purpose for man has not been fulfilled until he has been born of the Spirit! This assertion moves the new birth out of the area of life's options to the place of focal concern. Method and mode are not particularly important, but each person stands in need of a radical and fundamental reorientation of life at the very center. There must be a confrontation with his need of reconciliation to God. There must be a transformation.

This change will have both subjective and objective implications. This is more than an intellectual assent to a system of principles. The will must come into play. There must be a faith-response of repentance (new direction) and a receiving by faith of grace (acceptance of God's unmerited love and forgiveness). With this act of saving faith, life assumes a new direction.

When we begin a discussion of the "New Birth," however, the skeptic is entitled to wonder if human nature can be changed. We know change is in the natural order. When friends whom you have not seen for many months, come to visit, your first comment to the children is usually, "My, how you've changed." But not only do children grow. All around us is process and change. Nothing in creation is fixed and static. Birth, growth, death, and rebirth is the cycle in the natural order.

But what of that thing we call human nature? Webster defines it as the essential qualities or peculiar attributes which constitute man. Can this be changed? A young man confessed that he was in the grip of a vicious habit. Then he added, "I've given up all hope of ever being able to change." But even as he made the assertion, you had the feeling that he wanted to be assured that he could gain a victory.

The Bible and church tradition have much to say about this matter. We shall examine four of the ideas. The *first* is found in Genesis 1:26 where we read: "Then God said, 'Let us make man in our image, after our likeness.' " Christian tradition has always affirmed that there is a divine spirit within man which we call "the image of God." One theologian has written, "It is not possible for my faith to be shaken by man, however low he may sink; for this faith is not grounded on what man thinks about man, but on what God thinks about him. . . . There has not been enough emphasis on man: there has not been emphasis on man to the point of affirming him in God." This is a vital distinction. Man may write off man as animalistic and of little significance but God says, "Let us make man in our image. . . ."

Scientists quite properly devote much effort to analyzing man. He is physically measured, socially evaluated, and mentally tested. But the spirit of man, which "the image of God" suggests, cannot be contained nor schematized. The life and spirit of man are not substantial realities which can be held in the hand and docketed and described. They can only be expressed and when expressed in relationship to the Creator, they give a man a glory and a distinctiveness.

We are born again only when we say yes to the highest and best that is within us, when the passions come under the rule of the divine, when the life of the flesh yields to the life of the Spirit. It has been said that there is only one question a man must decide: "Which of the two men that you necessarily are, do you most deeply want to perish in order that the other might wear the crown?" In William James's famed definition there also is this insight. In conversion, he says, the divided self "becomes unified . . . in consequence of its firmer hold upon religious realities." Being born again is not just finding an integrative philosophy of life; it is responding affirmatively to the highest that we know and doing this in relationship to a transcendent reality—God himself.

Shakespeare wrote: "What a piece of work is man! How noble in reason! How infinite in faculty! In form and moving how admirable! In action how like an angel! In apprehension how like a god! The beauty of the world—the paragon of animals!"

A few short years after Shakespeare's death, however, Blaise Pascal was born. In a dramatic phrase he emphasized another aspect of man's nature. He wrote: ". . . man, . . . what a monster, what chaos, what a subject of contradiction, what a prodigy! Judge of all things, yet an imbecile earthworm: depository of truth, yet a sewer of uncertainty and error: pride and refuse of the universe."

To our detriment, we sometimes overlook this aspect of man's nature. Our pride prevents us from looking at the harsh reality. It is one of the astonishing facts of our time that at the very point in history where we have been faced with the horrors of gas chambers, atomic destruction, and the liquidation of masses, we not only refuse to acknowledge the enormity of human evil but seriously entertain distortedly optimistic estimates of man.

The Apostle Paul speaks to this situation by affirming, "There is no distinction; since all have sinned and fall short of the glory of God." (Romans 3:22-23) Here, then, is the *second* thing we must consider about man. The Bible and Christian tradition say he is a fallen creature. There was a time when our understanding of sin was embedded in a theology which spoke of Adam and Eve as the parents of the human race who lived in a state of innocence, but their disobedience involved all of mankind in a separation from God. When the scientists came along with theories about man's evolutionary development, this seemed to dispel the old notions of a fall.

In our generation, however, theologians have rediscovered "original sin." They no longer optimistically predict man's inevitable rise to perfection. Man's inhumanity to man has too clearly documented depths of evil and currents of rebellion deep within each of us.

The psychologists add their word of confirmation. They say we are whirlpools of unresolved conflict. Just as most of an iceberg is hidden beneath the surface of the water, so most of our behavior finds its well-springs beneath the surface of our awareness. Residual in each of us is a vast set of contradictions, struggles, and unresolved tensions which occasionally erupt. Little wonder that the existentialists, whose philosophy so dominated our thought for two decades, should speak of man as unpredictable and unreliable.

The dramatists in recent years have contributed their description of man's condition. And they make it quite clear that they are convinced that there is a depravity about man that thwarts his best intentions. In Arthur Miller's "After the Fall," he describes our condition as a sequel to some mythic fall. The central character, in spite of his good intentions, had spoiled his own life and the lives of those involved with him. He was weighed down with a sense of his own pointlessness. He had fallen away from a divine intention, and this is the root of the human tragedy.

Christian faith makes clear that the human condition is not what it ought to be, what God intended it to be. Something is seriously wrong. A strong word is needed to describe it. That word is sin. The Bible and Christian tradition say that man is a sinner estranged from God.

Every thoughtful person is aware of the paradox of man's wretchedness and greatness. He can rise to the heights; he can descend to the depths. There is inward tension, contradiction, and conflict. Man is a jungle of inward turmoil and ambivalence. This pull between the two forces creates the dynamic of movement out of which growth and renewal can come. The *third* thing, therefore, that we must say about the nature of man is that it is in tension, never standing still, always in the process of becoming. Paul Tournier, the Swiss psychotherapist, writes: ". . . man in movement, continually undergoing change, a man living in history, unfolding from his birth until his death." For a long period the approach to the study of man was static. Modern psychology and Christian theology both affirm, however, that man is in movement but the direction is open.

Do you remember Kipling's great classic entitled "Letting the Jungle In." It is the story of a group of people who went into the jungle, made a cleared place, brought their stock, planted their crops, and built their homes. For awhile it was a veritable paradise, until the rain years came and the jungle crept back. Wild animals killed their stock. The prolific vegetation of the jungle moved in faster than they could cope with it. The jungle took back their paradise. Of course, Kipling wasn't writing about the jungle at all. He was writing about man. He knew how near the jungle lies to the settlements of man, how thin is the veneer of civilization and how deep the savage in man. Our great upset at home and abroad today is but further evidence that Kipling was right. Today the beast, the jungle, the savage nature of man have suddenly begun to emerge again and it looks as if the jungle is about to take over again.

The meaning of the New Testament is that God has given us the help to turn back the jungle. St. John wrote, ". . . all who received him . . . he gave power to become children of God." (1:12) Man cannot conquer his perverse nature without divine help. There are those who, in moments of personal triumph, throw out the chest and shout, "I am the captain of my soul!" They believe salvation is for the weaklings. For a time this may work. But soon this make-believe world fades. And we are back to the same struggle which faced the Apostle Paul, there is a "warring within the members of the body."

T. Z. Koo, one of the great Chinese Christian leaders of this century, has often told what won him to Christianity in his student days. It was simply that Christianity came to him with a proposition different from that offered by any other religion. Confucianism, in which he grew up, was concerned only with ethics, only with the right and wrong of things, but Dr. Koo says that he did not find peace by simply trying to be a good man. In fact, the persistent sense of failure made him more wretched.

Then he heard about Christ, a Personality, who could enter life. He became a Christian, and to his surprise the ethical program followed. As he stood in a new relationship to God the old discouraging cry of "I ought" and "I must" was changed to the redeeming "I can" and "I will." When we are empowered by Christ, then we enter the realm of moral possibility.

This brings us to the *fourth* biblical statement about man. "Therefore, if any one is in Christ, he is a new creation." (2 Corinthians 5:17a) This is the heart of the matter. A Harlem pastor says, "I shudder when I hear Christians talk about meeting the real needs of men and then go on to list everything short of spiritual regeneration." God has acted in Christ to "break the power of cancelled sin" and restore us to a right relationship with himself. Leonard Griffith writes: ". . . Christianity has added a new rung to the ladder of evolution. Christianity has produced on this earth a new creature who lives in a new way to which the natural man can no more attain than a crawling thing can fly; a creature whose way of life is so radically different from what it has left behind that we can describe it by no other term than 'rebirth.' So if the question be asked objectively, 'How can a man be born when he is old?' it can be answered objectively, 'He is born through friendship with Jesus Christ.' "

The new birth is something more than a resolve, which needs repeated reenforcement, to respond to the greater good. It is the awareness that man is incapable of pulling himself up by his own goodness to approach unto God. Jesus went to the cross to make it clear that salvation is of God; we are forgiven and renewed and acceptable to God because of his action. This is the meaning of the parable of the prodigal son.

One year during the Lenten season I went to see a drama that portrayed the life of Jesus. "The Man Born to Be King" reached its climax in the crucifixion scene. The three Marys entered and approached the Roman guards. Mary, the mother of Jesus, spoke to the captain requesting permission to minister to the needs of her Son. He roughly pushed her away. Then one of the other women came forward and sought permission, adding: "For old times' sake." The guard refused her request. Then with a sweeping motion of her hand she loosed her golden hair so it could cascade down her back. "Marcellus," she asked, "have you ever seen hair like this?" And then she thrust out a foot and asked, "And have feet ever danced for you as these feet?"

Incredulity was on his face. In amazement he said: "Mary Magdalene, how you have changed!" Slowly, with dramatic emphasis, she turned so her back was to the audience and she was facing the cross and slowly said: "Yes, Marcellus, I have changed; he changed me."

This is what the new birth means. It means that all of us who were once aliens from divine favor can be accepted by a loving God as revealed in a cross. We can be released from the bondage of pretense and sin and become the persons God intends us to be. We are changed through accepting Christ as the One who reconciles God and man—the One who by his forgiving grace overcomes our estrangement.

To acknowledge Jesus as our Lord is to affirm that we belong to him. He is to rule in life. For years Augustine prayed that he might turn from his pagan ways and become a Christian. He even prayed, "Make me chaste." But he was living with a concubine, and his will always added to the prayer, ". . . but not now." New birth cannot take place when we consciously withhold areas of life from the control of Christ. To the rich young ruler Jesus said that he must rid himself of the lesser god in his life—his possessions—and surrender self to the lordship of Christ.

The tragedy of modern man's existence is not in the absurdities of life but in the absurd way in which he rebels against the commitment of his life to Christ. Saying yes to him is the conscious yielding of the whole self to God. No one would suggest this is an accomplishment easily achieved, but how foolish not to do so!

Self-assertion demands that we save ourselves through our own efforts rather than through surrender. The source of our salvation, however, is the universal atonement of Jesus Christ, and the channel by which the effects of this are brought to us is our faith. Both are merciful, undeserved gifts from God to the one who in humble repentance and believing faith says yes to Christ. This does not mean that every person will pass through an identical sort of experience, but whatever his experience, each person will be a true Christian.

In the middle of his life the great Russian, Leo Tolstoi, wrote, "Five years ago I came to believe in Christ and my life suddenly changed. I ceased to desire what I had previously desired and began to desire what I formerly did not want. . . . The direction of my life and my desires became different, and good and evil changed places."

How does all this happen? For some there is a sudden, spectacular experience which the embryologists call "condensed evolution." It is also true, however, that some of the most lasting, earth-shaking Christian conversions have taken place quietly, almost imperceptibly and over a long period of time, so that only in retrospect, only by looking back, as you look down a mountain to see how far you have climbed, do you realize the extent of the change in your life. How it happens we do not know except to say, God must do it.

John Wesley spoke of prevenient grace. Because of original sin, man is dead to God and unable to move toward him or respond to him. It is through prevenient grace that we are given the power to respond or resist. Only as God moves within our lives do we have the power to accept faith or refuse it.

The greatest of all the affirmative verses in the Bible is John 3:16. "God so loved . . . that he gave." This is the clue as to how God brings about the change in human nature.

8
SACRAMENTS

The Doctrinal Statement of the 1972 General Conference defines the church as "the sacramental community when, by adoration, proclamation, and self-sacrifice its members become conformed to Christ. Persons are initiated and incorporated into this community of faith by Baptism and Confirmation and accept their membership as confirmed by the Holy Spirit. By continuing celebration of the Lord's Supper, or Holy Communion, the church participates in the risen and present Body of Christ, being thereby nourished and strengthened by faithful discipleship. With churches of many traditions United Methodists affirm baptism and the Lord's Supper as the *two* principal sacraments given by God to his people."

The Roman Catholic Church, however, gives sacramental significance to seven of the many religious acts which were practiced in the early church—Baptism, Confirmation, the Holy Eucharist, Penance, Extreme Unction, Orders, and Matrimony. By way of contrast, the Quakers believe that the grace of God is immediate in the heart and feel no need for ritual acts as means of grace.

Important as we feel the sacraments are to the Christian

faith, it is well to remember that God cannot be limited and he may work with or without them. Clergymen must be careful lest they take themselves and the fact of whether or not one has received, for instance, tangible baptism too seriously. By this, of course, we mean the mechanical rite itself, not the fruit it produces. John Wesley stated it well in his *Letters*, III, 36: "You think the mode of baptism is 'necessary to salvation.' I deny that even baptism itself is so; if it were, every Quaker must be damned, which I can in no wise believe. I hold nothing to be (strictly speaking) necessary to salvation but the mind which was in Christ."

Nevertheless, baptism and the Lord's Supper have been a part of the life of the Christian Church since they were instituted by Jesus. The objects used in the sacraments all belong to the common life—water, bread, wine—but they set before us great unseen realities. As means of conveying God's grace, as symbols of God's creative and redemptive power and as memorials of what God has done for us through Jesus Christ, we do believe they are central to our life and faith.

What is a sacrament? It suggests something mysterious, beyond human understanding and knowledge, something sacred. The word itself, incidentally, comes from the Latin word "sacramentum" and was the word given to a sum deposited by two parties to a suit. Thus it suggests a covenant between God and man and has become, in the practice of the church, that formal moment when we celebrate the mystery of God and his covenantal relationship to his creature. It is, therefore, a dramatic reminder that God has done something: it is finished, accomplished. It is a symbol of his creative, redemptive power. We are reminded God has acted in our behalf. It is also an instrument through which God is now doing something. The action continues. Finally, in United Methodist understanding the effectiveness of the sacrament depends for its final fulfillment upon man doing something.

We turn now to an examination of the first idea that a sacrament is a reminder that God has acted in our behalf, has done something which is completed. The bread and wine say: "God's love has been sacrificially expressed in your behalf." Christ died on the cross for the sins of the world, and that includes you. It need not be done again. It was accomplished. Baptism reminds us that God granted his Holy Spirit for the renewal, cleansing, and transformation of man and established the church into which we may be incorporated. The sacraments, or ordinances, give visible assurance of God's presence and serve as signs of the initiative he has taken in the realm of our redemption. The divine acts form the objective element. God has acted, regardless of the response of man.

The sacraments are not only dramatic reminders of what God has done, but they are, in the second place, vehicles and instruments through which he is now doing something. They are pictures and symbols reminding us that God is coming to us now with forgiveness and saving help. In the Book of Acts there is no clear pattern, but it is plain that baptism was closely connected with the gift of the Spirit. Alone or with "Confirmation," it brought the gift. John 3:5 says, "Except a man be born of water and the Spirit, he cannot enter the Kingdom of God." It is impossible to state definitely whether the writer wishes to stress either of the two media, to the implied detriment if not the exclusion of the other, or whether he wishes to stress the necessity of both media. It would seem that "water and the Spirit" is one phrase which would suggest this is the way the early church understood baptism. If this is true, then baptism is thought of primarily as the gateway of the new birth. Something is happening now.

In this view the center of gravity is on rebirth to a spiritual life rather than on a remembered identification with Christ in his death and resurrection. Paul hints at this in 1 Corinthians 6:11 when he says of the Corinthian Christians, "Ye were washed, ye were sanctified, ye were justified, in the name of our Lord Jesus Christ, and in the Spirit of our God." For Paul, baptism was "into Christ," into union with him, into possession by him, into all the benefits, e.g. justification and sanctification, which flowed from being linked to him. Union with Christ involved sharing in his death and resurrection, of which baptism was an obvious sign and symbol. The Messianic age had dawned, and both Jew and Gentile could enter it by faith, the proof and expression of which was the acceptance of baptism. There was a new creature in a new creation. Baptism initiated converts into an organism. Thoughts such as these, particularly those associated with death and resurrection, suggest that baptism moved in the same circle of ideas as the Eucharist. Both were sacraments of union with Christ, leading to union with and in Christ's body. One was the sacrament of initiation; the other of continuing fellowship. The stress was on what it did for the believer now.

Compared with other church traditions in United Methodism, baptism as an external and visible act is given a secondary place and stress is laid on repentance, conversion, and justification, rather than on sacramental acts. This may reflect our heritage, coming from the revival movement, and emphasizing the personal conduct of the individual church member. It is significant, for instance, that Wesley in his amended version of the Thirty-Nine Articles of Religion replaced Article XVI "Of Sin After Baptism" by "Of Sin After Justification" (Article XII). This emphasis is reflected in the questions put to adults at the time of baptism: "Do you truly and earnestly repent of your sins and accept Jesus Christ as your Savior?" and "Will you obediently keep God's holy will and commandments and walk in the same all the days of your life?"

When the candidate has answered these questions, the minister then addresses the congregation: ". . . will you endeavor so to live that he may grow in the knowledge and love of

God the Father through our Lord Jesus Christ?" and the congregation is to respond: "With God's help we will so order our lives after the example of Christ that, surrounded by steadfast love, you may be established in the faith, and confirmed and strengthened in the way that leads to life eternal." These questions show the importance, in United Methodism, attached to admission and integration into the community of the faithful. In fact, the introductory statement of the minister is an invitation to the congregation to pray that God, "of his bounteous goodness will grant unto this person (that he) may receive the forgiveness of sins, be baptized with water and the Holy Spirit, and may be received into Christ's holy Church, and be made a living member of the same."

In other words, it is an act of dedication to God and to his will and purpose for our lives. It is also an act of initiation, by which we are grafted to the Body of Christ. It is, in summary, an act of spiritual new life and an identification with Christ's death and resurrection.

The third idea is our conviction that the effectiveness depends upon man doing something. We do not insist upon any one form of baptism. There are three principal modes: sprinkling, pouring, and immersion. Every adult and the parents of every child to be baptized have the choice. The reason for this flexibility is our belief that the amount of water used is not important. There was a time in Christian history when baptism was thought to have magical powers. The water was believed to have regenerating power of itself, if it had been consecrated by ritualistic words and made "holy water." From our point of view, the application of water does not change the nature of a person. It is easy to lapse into superstition. Parents who want a child baptized, but never attend church nor teach the Christian faith in the home, illustrate this. Nor can the application of water remove the curse of man's sin and impart a new nature and character. An ocean of water cannot effect a spiritual change. No sacred words or symbolic acts can make a person a disciple. Mode, in our judgement, and again stressing the subjective, is not as important as meaning and faith. We do not believe that the water has the power either to save or to damn. What the act does depends upon the inward response.

As one of our leaders reminds us, "Baptism is not the new birth, it is not regeneration, but it does save us, it does start us on the road to sanctification: if we repent, if we live in response to Christ's claim upon our lives, if we believe with heart, soul, mind, and strength, and if we obey the gospel's demand upon our lives. But if these assumptions and expectations are not fulfilled then our baptism is not valid and has no saving power in itself. . . ." What we are trying to say is that the sacraments are one of the means by which God comes to us with his forgiveness and saving help but freedom is at the heart of it. There is nothing coercive. It is finally a free meeting of spirit with Spirit. God comes with his grace and help but man must respond in faith and obedience. Even in infant baptism the child must finally claim for himself in the years of his maturity the covenant relationship with God if the relationship is to be sealed and made complete.

The validity of the sacrament depends finally, upon the inward response to the outward symbol. Preaching does not save the world else the world would have been saved long ago. A sermon saves in the measure that the hearer responds to the message by applying it to his own life. And so with baptism. We read in the Gospel that except a man be born of water and the spirit, he cannot enter the kingdom of God. Water alone does not save but if accompanied by an earnest resolution to live a Christ-committed life, baptism can be a means of Grace.

Then, you may ask, why do we baptize infants? Because if baptism is recognition of membership in the family of God, then it is natural for parents to want their children to receive this sign of being a part of God's kingdom. And by this act they acknowledge their thanksgiving for child life, they dedicate the child to the plan and purpose of God, and they vow to rear the youngster in the nurture of the faith so that when arriving at the years of discretion the child can make for himself the response of faith.

No church, to my knowledge, that baptizes infants, makes baptism equivalent to church membership. There is a second ceremony, known as confirmation, when at a later age the baptized person reaffirms for himself the vow which his parents took on his behalf at baptism. Every denomination that baptizes has two requirements for church membership: baptism and the taking of vows of discipleship. The churches that emphasize adult baptism meet the two requirements at the same time.

As to the further meanings of infant baptism, we do not view this as creating a new condition. We do not teach that the nature of the child is so polluted that if the youngster should die he would be lost forever. We are reluctant to suggest that baptism is a cleansing from the corruption of original sin.

Neither is it just a sweet ceremony. There is something about a child that attracts attention. Brides are often cautioned when planning a wedding that if they have a flower girl they must accept the fact that the youngster will probably receive more attention than the bride! And when parents present a child in a service of worship for the sacrament of baptism, every eye is directed toward the youngster. Baptism, however, is much more than a sweet and sentimental occasion. For this reason we suggest that this important sacrament not be sentimentalized by the use of a flower dipped into water and placed on the infant's head. This has no historic significance and cannot take the place of the hand of the minister placed directly upon the infant's head as a symbol that life is lived under the care and providence of God. As has been suggested, "We are dealing here with a profound spiritual mystery, not a touching ceremony."

One United Methodist theologian has summarized the cause of infant baptism by saying we observe this practice "because by birth God has set his mark and seal on each little child and claimed him for himself and his people." Because also God's mighty redemptive work in Jesus Christ has already been done in behalf of each infant and the Church celebrates that fact. Again, we believe in infant baptism because the whole community of faith, along with the family, needs to lift up each little child and claim him for Christ and his Church in advance of the age of accountability. In all things, including religion, the infant goes with the family.

The ritual reminds us that infant baptism is "an outward and visible sign of the grace of the Lord Jesus Christ, through which grace we become partakers of his righteousness and heirs of life eternal." The child presented in baptism is acknowledged as a part of the kingdom of love and care.

"Those receiving the sacrament are thereby marked as Christian disciples, and initiated into the fellowship of Christ's holy Church. Our Lord has expressly given to little children a place among the people of God. . . ." This is what our liturgy and practice affirm.

We baptize children recognizing that of such is the kingdom of God, and that they are already a part of God's kingdom of love and care and are entitled to baptism which is the outward sign.

We are all God's children by birth. Baptism is the visible witness of this in the face of an often forgetful world. Baptism does not make a person a child of God, but it is a public declaration of the fact that he is already a child of God.

The coronation did not make Elizabeth II the monarch of Britain, for coronation can only make a person a sovereign who is a sovereign already. It is the public declaration of a fact which already existed. A nation says: "This person is of royal lineage—put the crown on her head." The Church says: "This person is a child of God—baptize him."

It is also an opportunity for parents to dramatize their faith that they believe their child is not only physical and mental but spiritual and they have a responsibility to care for all aspects of his nature. The question they are asked reads: "Do you therefore accept as your bounden duty and privilege to live before this child a life that becomes the Gospel (and) will you endeavor to keep this child under the ministry and guidance of the Church until he by the power of God shall accept for himself the gift of salvation and be confirmed as a full and responsible member of Christ's Holy Church?"

They, the sponsors, and the Christian community, are confessing a responsibility for the spiritual nurture of this youngster in the devout hope and expectation that when able, he will "take for himself" a measure of responsibility for his deepening relationship with God.

There are those, of course, who raise questions about the authority for baptizing infants. Certainly the Bible does not command it nor forbid it. It is a practice that grew up very early in the Church. While probably it did not become universal until later—the first Church was principally an adult Church—there are references in the New Testament even of men and women baptized with their "households" (Acts 16:15, 33; 1 Corinthians 1:16), which certainly would not exclude children. During the second century, the Church Fathers referred to the practice of infant baptism as "apostolic" and to those who "had been made disciples from childhood." But whatever the weight of scriptural evidence or early practice, it is appropriate that parents and the believing community should want their children baptized in recognition of their membership in the family of God. And the Church could not refuse them, when our Lord took "the little ones" in his arms and blessed them (Mark 10:16). Also, as someone suggested, it is good wisdom to start the child right, in the company of Christ and his followers. Dramatic though the rescue of prodigals may be, it is better in the economy of the kingdom for the children never to leave the Father's house. Baptism is preventive medicine at the spiritual level.

The sacrament of the Lord's Supper is just as rich in meaning as baptism but more easily understood in United Methodist practice. It relates, of course, to the last supper which Jesus ate with his disciples (1 Corinthians 11:23-25). In the early church, before the ceremonial rite celebrated apart from the meal had developed, the followers of Christ met to have a meal together in memory of the event. They called it the "love-feast," a term which reminded them of the warmth of their fellowship in Christ. Much of this idea is suggested by our present word "communion." When we say "holy communion" we are recognizing its sacredness. In some denominations it is called the "Eucharist" which means thanksgiving, from the thanks which Jesus expressed when he took the bread and the cup in the Last Supper.

The Last Supper is a sacrament by which God comes to us reminding us of what he has done in the gift of his only begotten Son. It is a memorial service. The whole story of his suffering, death, and resurrection for our sakes is brought to our attention. "My body . . . given for you . . . do this in remembrance." United Methodists tend to stress the memorial aspects, the remembering, the recollection of Jesus.

It is also a time when God is doing something within us. The invitation calls for repentance from sin, an expression of love toward our neighbors, and the will to lead a new life according to the commandments of God. This call to repentance is followed by confession and a petition for forgiveness.

We do not believe that by some physical miracle the bread and wine have become the actual body and blood of Christ.

We must not neglect the emphasis, however, that Christ was given for our sins. In receiving the elements of remembrance, we can enter then into the newness of life. That is why there is a stress on confession, penitence, and dedication. As the drama of Christ's death and the assurance of his loving presence are reenacted, lives can be quickened, and our wills renewed. As one of our United Methodist theologians reminds us, "Through the bread and wine and symbolic acts, the death of Christ ceases to be merely past history and becomes a present, saving power in the lives of the worshippers."

There is also a rich quality of fellowship inherent in the practice of this sacrament. It is not a solitary act, it is "communion." We have fellowship with the disciples, martyrs, and the fathers of the faith. We do not believe in the "cafeteria concept" where the worshipper comes alone and helps himself. This sacrament is a visible, meaningful sign instituted by Christ and performed by the historical church acting through recognized ministers or by agents who intend to act for the church. You might distribute to your own family broken bread and the fruit of the vine and it would have rich devotional significance but for the sacramental character to be recognized we feel that the qualities of the church and recognized agents who act for the church must be present forming that link with the "choir invisible."

There is also a recognition that we must be in love and charity with our neighbors. Taking bread together can give us a sense of fellowship. This is not only with the person in the pew but with those who are followers of the Christ all around the world. This is why we frequently take an offering for "others" on "World-wide Communion Sunday." We are made to think of that great company of Christians of all ages who have remembered the Christ. It gives us a lifting sense of the reality of the "communion of saints."

Included in this fellowship is our doctrine of the "real presence" of Christ. When we come to the table of the Lord in the Spirit of Christ, we find him there. "Do this in remembrance of me" and he is there. "Lo, I am with you always" is the rich promise. What a beautiful sight it is to see Christian people kneeling together, receiving the elements, and in deep communion with their neighbors, their fellow-believers all over the world, and with the Christ.

There is one more aspect of this sacrament that needs to be mentioned. It is a reminder that all life is sacramental. When we use the common elements of bread, the staff of life, and the fruit of the vine which in Jesus' day was the common drink, we are saying that all life is sacramental. The common things of life can be used as a symbol of the spiritual. The world about us can be the instrument by which God comes to us. The humble tasks in which all of us engage as we go about our daily round should be the links which bind us to God. And in this spirit we can, while kneeling at the sacrament, offer our lives to God each day.

9
PRAYER

United Methodists have always stressed the personal, the subjective, the experiential. We believe in person-to-person communion with God. We believe it is possible to have a genuine awareness of the greatness, glory, mystery, and love of God. This is based on our conviction that God, the Creator and Sustainer, is approachable. Our Doctrinal Statement affirms "Life in the Spirit means . . . the life of prayer and inward searching; it also involves . . . the communal life of the church." When Wesley formed the societies he defined their purpose by saying a society is no other than "a company of men having the form and seeking the power of godliness, united in order to pray together, to receive the word of exhortation, and to watch over one another in love, that they may help each other to work out their salvation." He also spoke of the "ordinances of God" which included "family and private prayer."

Many things are hard to explain. One of these is prayer. At best our explanations are halting and awkward. We don't however, omit prayer because we can't understand its full meaning. Jesus himself demonstrated this in his use of prayer. He made no effort to argue or analyze the subject. As he assumed the existence of God, so he also assumed the naturalness of prayer. He did not raise nor answer the problems which weigh so heavily upon educated men today. He lived in an age when nearly all people believed in prayer and most practiced at least the outward forms. But our generation does not take prayer as seriously. There may be many reasons.

It could be because of the overpowering influence of secularism. In a world of scientific certainty and mathematical probability, why pray? As one young college student said, "Science does not deny God; she goes one better; she makes him unnecessary!" It could be that we have ceased to believe in a God who pays attention to prayer. Professor Altizer, of "God Is Dead" notoriety, wrote in one of his articles: "Surely no responsible person any longer believes that it is possible to know or experience God in anything that is genuinely modern."

To pray effectively requires certain beliefs. We must first believe that prayer has value. Alfred Lord Tennyson once wrote that "more things are wrought by prayer than this world dreams of."

Does prayer really make a difference, or is it just good therapy? The Apostle James wrote, "The effectual fervent prayer of a righteous man availeth much." (James 5:16) In the very next verse he says, "Elijah was a man subject to like passions as we are, and he prayed earnestly that it might not rain: and it rained not on the earth by the space of three years and six months. And he prayed again, and the heavens gave rain. . . ." Take special note of the phrase, "a man subject to like passions as we are." But an examination of his life reveals that when he had a need, he knew that God was the source of supply. He then prayed earnestly. He prayed in faith and an answer came. Effectual prayer involves a conviction that it has limitless possibilities for renewal, guidance, and power.

No man will pray unless he has become persuaded it can make a difference.

The second necessary belief is the conviction that there is an interior life which must be cultivated. General Charles de Gaulle has been quoted as saying, "Man wants to travel to the moon. That is not far enough. He must first travel to the depths of his own soul." There is an echo in that phrase of the scriptural passage which says, "For what will it profit a man, if he gains the whole world and forfeits his own soul?"

The great discoveries of the next decades will hopefully be in the mental and spiritual realm. This is our only hope for remaining truly human, for if our spiritual advances don't keep pace with our technology, then we are doomed! We must develop, sensitize, and strengthen life's inner resources. The late C. G. Jung, a one time disciple of Freud, said that the individual who is not anchored in God can offer no resistance of his own resources to the physical and moral blandishments of the world. Only as we have concluded that "man cannot live by bread alone" will we devote the necessary energy and effort the spiritual cultivation requires. It is, however, the great imperative of our generation.

The third required belief is a firm conviction that the theistic position is valid. By this I simply mean a belief, rooted in faith and experience, that God is personally interested in what happens to us and will not abandon that which he has created.

The Christian faith has always taught that prayer is a two-way communication between ourselves and the God whom Jesus came to reveal and to serve, and it must be stated as clearly as possible that unless one does believe in God, there is nothing left to say about prayer. Prayer is not talking to ourselves; it is not simply cajoling ourselves into a better frame of mind. It is standing on the solid ground of God's omnipotent goodness.

Let us now examine the three major dimensions of prayer

as understood by United Methodists. *First*, it is private, personal, and mystical. It is the ascent leading toward the vision of God. It is communion with the Creator, Sustainer, and Empowerer of our lives. It is receiving the blessings and benefits which God has for us.

This is accomplished in many ways. It is reading and reflecting on the Word of God. The spiritual masters have a disciplined pattern of time and place for the encounter with God. We may not have this, but all of us can use the moments of solitude that present themselves for reflection and brooding. The word brooding has a bad image. It connotes a low-grade distemper, meditative melancholy, the power of negative thinking. But this is unfair to brooding, which, as any hen knows, can be a most productive experience. It's the sort of "sitting on an idea" that often yields fresh insight. It's the kind of fruitful pondering a man may do in the solitude of early morning or late evening, or when protected by the anonymity of a commuter train or bus. This thought, coming from a book by Robert Raines, *Creative Brooding*, reminds us that all around are selections from the newspaper, the magazines, plays, poets, and the Bible, which can be used for reflection and prayer. Such reflection should shake the foundations, awake thought, and precipitate action.

Marcus Aurelius once observed that weak men seek retreats whereas strong men carry theirs with them. To nurture within oneself a resource to turn to—a place to go—toughens the fiber and expands the horizons of the human spirit. Self-pitying isolation must be avoided but creative aloneness provides an essential place of rest and renewal on our journey toward worthy selfhood. There is no cure for self-centered loneliness comparable to a life shared with the Eternal.

Another thing we can do is to use our imagination. The mind is active all the time. The imagination moves in many directions. Cultivate the habit of making it work for you. In Mark 11:24 we read, "Whatever you ask in prayer, believe that you receive it, and you will." The Bible also reminds us that as a man thinketh, so is he. All this suggests the importance of the mind and imagination.

Many psychologists regard the imagination as more powerful than the will. They believe that if the will is set in one direction but the imagination is firmly held in another, the imagination will ultimately win. Employ the imagination in prayer. Picture yourself already possessing the graces you desire. Picture the prayer fulfilled. Link imagination with affirmation. Hold in your mind the image of yourself made anew in Christ. See it with clarity and conviction. See the fearful you, truly trusting—the resentful you, fully forgiving.

Someone has said that all of us carry on a constant dialogue with ourselves. We shall be reluctant to place too much emphasis upon the "power of positive thinking," but there is truth here that can be ignored only at our own risk. We know there is power in negative thinking. "As a man thinketh, so is he." There is power in these words. So think the best, the highest, the noblest, about yourself and others for such thoughts, such imaginations, have a way of becoming self-fulfilling.

We must realize, of course, that prayer as communion with God is much more than reflection or the creative use of the imagination. This may suggest how we can creatively use available resources for praying, but it is also a "person-to-person" communion with God. It is a meeting of "Spirit with spirit." What this is cannot be adequately defined nor described. It must be experienced.

Harry Emerson Fosdick, in his autobiography, tells that when he was a young preacher he suffered a severe nervous breakdown. This was followed by a period of bitter depression. "For the first time in my life," he wrote, "I faced, at my wit's end, a situation too much for me to handle. I went down into the depths where self-confidence becomes ludicrous. . . . In that experience I learned some things about religion that theological seminaries do not teach. I learned to pray, not because I had adequately argued out prayer's rationality, but because I desperately needed help from a Power greater than my own. I learned that God, much more than a theological proposition, is an immediately available Resource." What an exciting discovery to make!

The *second* dimension of prayer for us is the linking of piety with social action. Before leaping into the battle to correct injustice, we should gain the "mind of Christ." When we understand that we are doing his work, we have a sustaining motivational power.

A little girl came home from school with pride over what she had learned that day. She was eager to tell someone. "Daddy," she exclaimed eagerly, "I learned what the earth does every twenty-four hours." "What does it do, honey?" dutifully asked her father. "It revolts on its abscess," was the quick answer. Well, there is a sickness that has laid its hands upon our world. Needs are so urgent. There is so much to do. And people of prayer must also act.

The venerable Albert Schweitzer, in his declining years, was asked by a reporter about the world's distress. Schweitzer shared with him his philosophy: "No matter how great the evil of the world, I always hold firmly to the conviction that each of us can do something to bring some portion of that evil to an end." Our prayer should be, "Lord, show me what I can do about the world's evil."

Piety without social concern is incomplete. When Francis of Assisi prayed for the lepers of Italy, it occurred to him that God expected him to do more than pray, so he went and

lived with them. He lavished care upon them, dressed their
wounds, and became one with them in their sufferings.

. One of our greatest assets in the struggle with evil is to
live a life of faith and integrity. This confirms our witness
for truth and equity. We need to pray about our decisions.
God will make available to the inner consciousness a wisdom
greater than our own. He will make his will known to us if
we wait and listen.

There's an old story preachers tell of a minister who was
invited to another church at a considerable increase in salary.
He did not know if he should go and was devoting much time
to prayer. One day a parishioner saw his small son on the
sidewalk and asked what his daddy was going to do. The
youngster replied, "Well, Father's praying, but Mother's pack-
ing!" In many of our decisions the desire for reward, the fear
of punishment, or the love of self intrude and prevent the
accomplishment of God's will. We need divine wisdom as we
try to make decisions and render choices.

We need to pray about the moral sag in life. Jesus recognized
that we struggle with evil. He spoke of temptation. He noted
that we often need to pray the prayer for forgiveness. All of
us need strength to resist the wrong. A young serviceman, home
on furlough, was talking with his pastor, who asked what the
church should be doing for its young people. The answer was
unexpected. The young soldier said, "I think the church ought
to be teaching young people how to pray." His army experience
had placed him in some difficult situations. He had found that
the deeper spiritual resources were not there when he needed
them. In the struggle for moral mastery, he had gone down
to defeat.

The *third* dimension of prayer for United Methodists grows
out of our conviction that we should pray for others. We do
believe in intercessory prayer. Jesus prayed for others. By
example, Jesus taught his disciples to pray for each other. Paul

and others persisted in this practice. Every church should have intercessory prayer groups who lift the needs of each other, and of the world, to the throne of God's mercy. "No man is an Iland, intire of it selfe," John Donne reminds us. Each person is a part of the mainland of humanity, a member of the human family, an integral part of the divine-human community. As such, each person is related to others and depends upon others for his very existence.

This sense of being related to others gives validity to our prayers. Dr. Edward Bauman writes: "When we pray for others we are holding their lives up before God so that his light may shine upon them. We are seeking to influence them to open their lives to God. In turn, we are strengthened by the prayers of others in our moments of deepest distress. This mutual influence, which comes from prayer, is similar to other influences arising out of the social nature of our existence. Such prayer helps to break down the barriers that separate men from one another, barriers that often lead to increased misunderstanding. Modern science and industry have done a great deal to overcome barriers of time and distance, but many people still face each other across formidable obstacles of race and religion, of interest and education, of ideas and ideals. Unable to communicate and cooperate because of such obstacles, persons often find themselves unwillingly involved in incidents of hatred and bloodshed. How different the situation is when men are sincerely praying for one another! William Law emphasized this value of intercession in strengthening community relationships when he said, "There is nothing that makes us love a man so much as praying for him. . . ."

Praying is sometimes all we can do for one another. Frank Laubach, the literacy expert, dedicated a book with these words: "To all who are dissatisfied with what they are doing for the world." If we feel discontent that we cannot do more about world problems, then let us pray!

Actually, we have a sacred responsibility at this point. We often cite our Protestant heritage with its magnificent phrase, "The priesthood of all believers." This does not just mean that we have the privilege of approaching God directly. It means that the priest's approach to God is made on behalf of others. With the privilege of being a priest comes the sacred responsibility of practicing that priesthood in order to bring others into the light of God's love. So even though we are tied down by responsibilities in home and business, or weakened through sickness and disability, we can still pray. Every shut-in can still have a ministry. No person is too busy to deny himself this ministry of prayer. All must practice their "priesthood" which means intercession for others. But we may appropriately ask how intercession for another "works." One suggestion is found in the development of an idea by the late Leslie Weatherhead. He has written:

> Telepathy is the communication of ideas from one mind to another without the use of the senses. In my opinion, the evidence for it is conclusive. It seems to me a fact that in certain circumstances minds which are on the same "wave-length," and especially when they are under the stress of some benign emotion, do at times communicate messages to one another, geographical distance making no difference.

What beauteous insight we have here. When Paul said, "We have not ceased to pray for you," this may have been in part what he had in mind. We can touch another person on the unconscious level. And isn't this what a group is doing when they pray for another?

We certainly do not wish to imply that prayer is only telepathy. This would be the same mistake of an earlier generation who felt that evolution negated the idea of God's creative power. Actually, all evolution does is describe the creative process. In similar fashion, telepathy only describes the mental machinery by which God uses, in some cases, our intercession for our friends.

Praying for people has always puzzled us. We pray for one person, and he recovers. We pray for another and he dies. The cynic might say that one person would have recovered anyway. There are no easy answers.

The Christian, however, will continue to pray for he is under command. "He told them a parable to illustrate the truth that they ought always to pray and not lose heart." (Luke 18:1) Furthermore, Christ himself prayed for others, and we cannot refuse to follow his example. Most of us, having faced our obligation to pray for others, seek some guidance and instruction as to how we proceed with this ministry of prayer. First, we are to be specific in our request—confess our needs, express our desires. Jesus did this when praying in the Garden of Gethsemane. He agonized, "Remove this cup from me."

Make clear what we desire. "Man tells what he desires," says Luther. "He is not abashed before exalted Majesty, but speaks outright." John Calvin believed that prayer was insti- tuted in order that "we may confess our needs to God and bring him our complaints as children bring their grievances confidently to their parents.

Then, we must always make these requests, however specific, in the spirit and name of Christ who prayed, "Thy will be done." There are many times when we have wanted something very earnestly only to discover years later it would not have been to our advantage to have received our request. Our knowl- edge is finite and limited. Every petition must conclude with the phrase, "Thy will be done."

One of the best illustrations of how to pray is found in this incident. Howard Thurman has told of a ninety-year-old woman who had been a member of a certain church for more than fifty years. Her present minister was not loved by the people,

but he insisted on staying despite all efforts to have him re-
moved. This elderly woman took an entire afternoon to pray
about this difficult situation. She began with the day she joined
the church and unhurriedly reviewed fifty years of her own
life in relation to the church. She then went into great detail,
explaining to the Lord all about the minister, the people, and
the present crisis. When she finished, she said, "Now Lord,
I have given you all the facts. Take them and do the best
you can. I have no suggestion to make."

As we deepen our skills in prayer, we will be moved to
pray less for material and temporal things and more for spiritual
wishes. The Apostle Paul has given us an example of this. He
asked God to give his friends such things as spiritual strength,
unity, certainty, knowledge, and love. In telling them about
his prayers, he reported having asked "that the name of our
Lord Jesus may be glorified in you," "that you may not do
wrong," "that you may be saved."

Notice the kind of petitions Jesus offers in his intercessory
prayer for his disciples. He asked the Father to "keep them
in thy name." He asked that they be "sanctified in truth."
He petitioned, "Don't take them out of the world, but keep
them from the evil one." That is, he did not pray that the
disciples would have it easy. He did pray that they would
be able to withstand the evils and temptations of this present
world. Gandhi said that our prayers for others should be, "Give
them all the light and truth they need for their highest development."

10
FAITH AND WORKS

The Doctrinal Statement of the 1972 General Conference says that "perhaps the most widely cherished doctrinal emphasis among United Methodists is that faith and good works belong together. Guided by the Spirit, our understanding swings between two poles. On the one side, faith is intensely personal ('Christ is my Savior'; 'Christ for *us!*'). On the other side, as The General Rules remind us, this inward assurance, if genuine, is bound to show itself outwardly in good works. By joining heart and hand, United Methodists have stressed that personal salvation leads always to involvement in Christian mission in the world. Thus we assert that personal religion, evangelical witness, and Christian social action are reciprocal and mutually reinforcing."

One of our theologians expresses his understanding of this passage by saying, "We United Methodists continue to urge upon the contemporary world the need for the kinds of inner transformation, growth, and insight which, with the power of the Holy Spirit, necessarily issue in the responsible management of life, both personally and socially. The formula is: from inner transformation of heart and mind to creative leadership and authentic social reform." This is a splendid affirmation of the conviction that has always stood at the center of the church's teaching that faith and fruit must be linked.

Our fathers set the example for us. In fact, the very name "Methodist" stems from the fact that Wesley and the others who shared with him in the Oxford Holy Club were "methodical" not only in the practice of their devotions but also in the accomplishment of various acts of charity including working for penal reform. We must remember that Christianity is a materialistic religion. It is concerned with this world. Jesus prayed, "Thy will be done on earth. . . ." Christianity is not something that goes on once a week in a building we call a church. It is a way of life, a style of living. It is the total context in which we live and move and have our being. It is a way of thinking, of speaking, of acting. It has to do with home, school, community, politics, business—as well as church. The real authority of the church is an example. As an institution the church may be shorn of prestige and power. This could happen in our generation. The apostolic church, though a persecuted and dispossessed minority group, lived and grew in the power of the Holy Spirit. They were able to love one another and render no man evil. This showed the world a better way than that of hate and oppression. This proclaimed a message that survived the defeat of armies and the collapse of empires. When faith and fruit become joined, nothing can shake the church.

It is our desire to examine two questions that are urged upon us for answer. *First,* do the sacred and secular ever mix, or in practical but more emotional terms, do politics and religion ever belong together? The second question will be concerned with the prophetic role in our decade.

During the first sixteen hundred years of church history the question of mixing politics and religion would have aroused little interest because the answer would have been an obvious yes. In western civilization, church and state were usually wedded. More recently, in England, Italy, Israel, Pakistan, and numerous other countries the link between state and church is openly acknowledged.

Our own Pilgrim fathers assumed they would be conjoined. But in time they discovered, as did John Calvin in Geneva, that a church invested with national authority can become oppressive. The witch-hunt was the more dramatic form this took in our own history.

Finally, through the efforts of many persons, notably Roger Williams, who played a role in the establishment of Rhode Island, the idea of the separation of Church and State was accepted. Historians have called this the GREAT EXPERIENCE. Many of us, as youngsters working puzzles, learned the long word ANTIDISESTABLISHMENTARIANISM which simply meant you were against separation of church and state.

By the time of the writing of the Constitution, the pluralistic character of our society was apparent; and it is a part of our national life that Congress shall make no law respecting the establishment of religion. This is not designed to be anti-religion. It means the state shall not dominate the church as it did in Nazi Germany and now in Russia, nor should the church dominate the state as it did for several centuries in Italy. Nor does it prevent the national government from being concerned about the church. We do not pay taxes on the building in which we meet for worship; clergy are exempt from the selective service.

And the church is not prevented from making its point of view known. The first amendment supports the right of citizens to "petition the government for redress of grievances." If the church officially becomes a lobby, however, it can lose its tax-exempt status. What is the situation today?

There is the attitude of complete separation. In 1967 an

organization known as "Clergymen and Laymen Concerned About Vietnam" asked ministers and laymen to go to Washington and call on their congressmen. One minister wrote to his congressman saying, "I will not be among them. I will stay at home and preach the gospel." But those who stayed home and preached the gospel had to be concerned about the welfare situation in their city, the quality of public education, the rights of minorities, and all the other issues that make for human betterment. None of us believe that preaching the gospel is just saving a soul with no concern for the quality of his present life.

Another point of view is that the church must make its voice felt on issues that directly affect the church and its activities such as opportunity for missions, freedom of speech as it pertains to radio and evangelism, and the sending of ambassadors or envoys to the Vatican. They would insist that only when the state infringes on a citizen's responsibility to God does the citizen have the right to defy the state.

The third point of view, taken by most United Methodists, is expressed by one senator who has said, "Every political question is a moral question, which challenges politicians to seek the guidance of the church." This view would say that most public issues have religious implications. Aristotle defined politics as the art of making and keeping people truly human. Therefore, the Christian gospel must have something to say about the social, economic, and political affairs of man as well as his spiritual needs. By way of historic precedent John Wesley once said, "We have nothing to do but save souls," but he also said, "I have no religion but a social religion." And the revival of which he was a part made a unique contribution to the abolition of the slave trade, prison reform, and the birth and development of the labor party.

At the same time, the church and the individual Christian must practice humility. When some individual of limited experience offers a statement which would resolve war, eliminate poverty, and remove racism in one paragraph and then indicts everyone who doesn't embrace his point of view, we wonder about both his intelligence and integrity. The majority of people in politics are honorable, hardworking public servants who sincerely want to do a good job and probably have more experience than most who sit outside. We are often embarrassed by the self-righteous expressions and intolerant opinions of some churchmen.

There may come an occasional moment when the church as an institution must rise up and say to the state that it is not God; that its goals must be reexamined in the uncomfortable glare of biblical morality. There comes an occasional moment when the church as an institution must remind persons even in high places that they also stand under the judgment of God. We may not know how to offer political and military advice, but we can and must, on occasion, express moral outrage.

Albert Einstein, in an oft-quoted statement printed in the *New York Times,* said:

> As a lover of freedom, when the revolution came in Germany, I looked to the universities to defend it, knowing that they had always boasted of their devotion to the cause of truth; but no, the universities were immediately silenced. Then I looked to the great editors of the newspapers, whose flaming editorials in days gone by had proclaimed their love of freedom; but they, like the universities were silenced in a few short weeks. Only the church stood squarely across the path of Hitler's campaign for suppressing truth. I never had any special interest in the church before, but now I feel a great affection and admiration for it, because the church alone has had the courage to stand for intellectual truth, and moral freedom. I am forced to confess that what I once despised, now I praise unreservedly.

The Church must speak because we believe that man's knowledge is partial; only God is omniscient. We will come closer to the truth if there is open discussion, debate, and honest, responsible difference of opinion. No leader is wise enough to foresee all the consequences of his action or to plan for every eventuality in the midst of complex and conflicting forces. We must have in a free society the equivalent of the British "loyal opposition."

Another reason for speaking out rests on the Christian assumption that all men are possessed of sinful tendencies and are inclined to seek power or prestige for its own sake. This power must be checked and safeguards established so that the will of no man or group is beyond having someone question it.

We also have the conviction, established by the Nuremberg Trials after World War II, that there is a law higher than that of any nation. Our judges refused to accept the German defense that they were only obeying the law of their land and were innocent of any wrong doing. Our officials appealed to a law higher than that of any nation and eliminated the normal appeals to the nature of war as justification for any act.

Let us consider the *second* question. This raises the issue of what it means to be "prophetic" in our kind of world. In the effort to put faith and good works together there may be a few admonitions to keep in mind. In the first place we must not pretend to have all the answers to the political and social ills that afflict our society. Jesus did not attempt to offer precise solutions for every issue. He demonstrated deep compassion for those in need but when asked about some political question he answered, "Render unto Caesar the things that belong to Caesar. . . ." Ordination does not qualify a man to make judgments concerning political, economic, or international affairs. An ordained person may qualify himself in these fields by study and experience, but then the prophetic character is determined not by his status as a clergyman but by his qualifications in these areas of concern. And always, we must remember that decisions in economics and politics have to be made ultimately by the men who actually bear the consequences of their decisions. We live in a democratic, pluralistic society. Men of equal Christian commitment and wisdom may disagree with respect to specific issues. We must, therefore, not say, "Thus saith the Lord." We can surely say, "This is the way I see it. This is my best judgment." But we must know there are other men, equally honest, equally able, who are committed to quite an opposite view.

Furthermore, the person who struggles to be "prophetic" is usually tempted to cite the example of the Old Testament prophets. While they were concerned about the social ills of the day, they were first of all trying to call their people back to a faith which was being neglected, misunderstood, and distorted. We often quote out of context Isaiah's famous vision of a world at peace: "They shall beat their swords into plowshares." But we neglect to mention that this universal peace is grounded in a vision of universal faith. It is only when the mountain of the Lord has been established that the nations will learn war no more.

There are all sorts of good deeds being accomplished out of splendid humanitarian motives. But the prophet is one who senses that righteousness is a result of religious revival. In a way, the person is right who insists that the preacher's first job is to talk about a man's relationship with God and from this new circumstance will come the motive to work on the social ills.

On one occasion they brought a paralytic to Jesus. He wanted to be healed. But Jesus first began talking about forgiving the man his sins. When some of his critics questioned his right to forgive sins, he answered by saying, "That you may know that I have power to forgive sins, I will command this man to take up his bed and walk." But his first concern was for the man's spiritual condition.

We must remember this. Much social reform is secular and humanistic. But we can feed people until they are fat, clothe them elegantly, house them luxuriously, but if they do not have faith, and a right relationship with the Creator of Life, then the prophet has failed.

The prophetic person will believe in the power of moral persuasion. If a man of faith doesn't believe in the ultimate victory of love, who will? Secular society responds to other forces. Recently the personnel director of a large corporation and two of his associates invited four clergymen to have lunch with them. They explained in some detail the Equal Employment Opportunity Policy of their company and described what they call their "Affirmative Action Program." They said they were now doing many things they were not doing five years ago. When asked what were the forces that brought about this change in climate the answer given was this: First, government action. Because the government expected certain hiring policies to prevail, they cooperated. Second, a period of full employment made it possible for them to dip down into what they would usually consider marginal groups; and third, the riots! Then the speaker continued, "I know you will be disappointed, but I don't think the church had much to do with it."

In other words, preaching brotherhood had not made much difference. But riots, the threat of burning down the town, brought some swift changes in the hiring practices of a company that has been noted for its progressive policies. Someone has pointed out, "Poor, hurt, hungry people have nothing to gain from silence. Nobody rewards them for orderly behavior, for quiet acquiescence, for suffering in obscurity. Endless patience brings them nothing." Often this is tragically true. Nevertheless, we recall that when Jesus rode into Jerusalem to bring into the open, through confrontation, the evil that was entrenched, he refused to permit Peter to take a sword. He was fearless;

he spoke out against hypocrisy. But he never used force except to drive the money changers out of the temple, and that is not a model for violence.

He was a revolutionary, but not in the sense of using violence. This is why the Jews rejected him. They wanted a military leader. He said, "Quit grumbling about the Roman occupation and win them through kindness." His method was often not so much civil disobedience as a kind of doubled-up civil obedience. Said he, "If any soldier of the occupation compels you to carry his equipment one mile, fool him, and carry it two!" But the whole style of his ministry was a rejection of actual violence.

In one of his speeches, Martin Luther King said: "The ultimate weakness of violence is that it is a descending spiral, begetting the very thing it seeks to destroy. Returning violence for violence multiplies violence, adding deeper darkness to a night already devoid of stars. Darkness cannot drive out darkness: Only light can do that. Hate cannot drive out hate: Only love can do that." The real prophet must not forget this! Yet there are times when the Christian must act. Norman Mailer wrote in an autobiographical sketch, "How poor to go to death with no more than the notes of good intention. It is the actions of men and not their sentiments which make history."

In the mid-forties, Nazi troops aroused Dietrich Bonhoeffer, marched him through the cool, springlike morning to the sandy courtyard, stripped him naked, and hanged him. Bonhoeffer was a quiet theologian, a pacifist, who loved his fatherland intensely. Yet he had involved himself in the assassination plot on Hitler and plotted the downfall of his country. In so doing, he felt he was obedient to God. He was a visiting professor at Union Theological Seminary when the war came, and he returned home against the advice of his friends. He felt he must do what he could to overthrow the Nazis so western civilization could be preserved. He defined Christ as the man for others—the one who suffered for his fellowman. He felt the church must suffer and sacrifice.

Jesus "went about doing good." He had what has been defined as the "posture of availability," but his actions were always out of love for God and man. This is the model for the contemporary prophet. Others may do it just because of a humanitarian impulse; the genuine prophet will do it out of love for God and man, and obedience to Christ.

11
ETERNAL LIFE

Dr. Kubler-Ross is a doctor who did an extensive study of the needs and attitudes of those who have terminal illness. In an address to ministers she indicated that as she conducted her interviews, she soon discovered that questions were being raised she did not feel qualified to answer. Patients wanted to know what follows death. She asked a group of theological students to assist her in seeing the patients. Strangely, they did not seem to be of much help. She called them together and asked: "How many of you, without any shadow of doubt, believe in life after death?" When put that way, no one seemed confident enough to raise a hand. "I then knew," she said, "why they were unable to help the patients with their questions about life after death. They were using the right phrases, but their own uncertainty was coming through in the interviews with the terminally ill patients."

This doubt, while prevalent, is not in keeping with our heritage which affirms the Life Everlasting. In the Doctrinal Statement we read: ". . . we gladly declare that the forgiveness of sins and life eternal are ours through the power of God's

invincible love . . . It is this love that defines our chief aim
in life: 'to glorify God and to enjoy him forever.' "

While this theme does not occupy as large a place in preaching and Christian education as once accorded to it, the fact
remains that central to Christian faith is the notion of eternal
life. Our hymnal is rich with symbolism that testifies to the
place of this theme in our corporate life. This is found not
only in hymns but in our liturgical expressions, such as the
Korean Creed, printed in our hymnal, which affirms: "We
believe in the final triumph of righteousness, and in the life
everlasting." The empty tomb and the life everlasting are
always a part of our proclamation when we are faithful to
the New Testament. The gospel, the "good news," is that God
has acted in our behalf at the point of our mortality. There
is the awesome reminder in Scripture that "It is appointed
unto man once to die. . . ." The reality of our finitude makes
us reach out for answers as to life's meaning. The span of life
is so short, and frequently so heavy with burden, that we yearn
for understanding and meaning and become convinced that
only from the perspective of eternity can we see clearly its
meaning.

Death comes to all men, and is sometimes a welcome visitor,
but what happens after death is a question that has haunted
the human mind at least as long as recorded history. One fairly
common belief is extinction. Death is the end. This inscription
was found on an ancient Roman tomb: "I was not, and then
I was born. Now, I am not and I care not."

Others believe in transmigration. This is notably true of some
of the eastern religions. According to this doctrine the soul
transmigrates up or down into another body living on this earth.
After death we may become a reptile or a prince. Our behavior
in this life destines our body in the next.

Others believe in absorption. At death we are lifted up into
one great prevailing spirit. Individual identity is lost. It is as

a drop of water that falls into the ocean. There is continued existence, but not on an individual basis.

The Christian faith, however, has always affirmed a self-conscious existence beyond this life. In the year A.D. 125, a Greek by the name of Aristodes wrote to one of his friends about the new religion, Christianity. He was trying to explain the reasons for its extraordinary success. Here is a sentence from one of his letters:

> If any righteous man among the Christians passes from the world, they rejoice and offer thanks to God and they escort his body with songs and thanksgiving as if he were setting out from one place to another nearby.

A man who had lived his entire life within the Church reached his eightieth birthday. At a dinner given him on that occasion, he arose and said:

> In my long life I have had many exciting adventures. I have crossed the ocean numerous times, and have been around the world. But I am awaiting the greatest adventure of all, the journey into that land from which no traveler has ever returned.

That is the sort of faith with which a Christian faces the end of his life.

Now what's the basis for this confidence, this mood of assurance? Let us acknowledge that we cannot accumulate physical evidence for survival of bodily death that becomes convincing proof.

Nor can we advance an undeniable chain of logical argument nor can we gain the kind of evidence that comes from weighing, counting, and measuring tangible things. But then there are remarkably few things that can be proved that way. Nothing can be proved about beauty, goodness, truth, honor, honesty, or love by these methods. Let us admit frankly that we are entering the realm of faith. And what we say is an attempt to reenforce the faith of the believing community. You can't persuade an unbeliever by argument. It can only be done by example and by his own hunger for certainty.

We advance four reasons for faith in the reality of continued self-conscious existence. The *first* reason is that there seems to be something in us that aspires after a life free of the mortal body.

For whatever reasons, sizeable numbers of the specimen "modern man" have not lost a propensity for awe, for the uncanny. In a study of American students, published by Princeton Press, while only 48 percent admitted to a belief in God in traditional Judaeo-Christian terms, 80 percent expressed a "need for religious faith." In a similar study in Germany, while only 68 percent said they believed in God, 86 percent admitted to praying on occasion.

Peter Berger, a noted sociologist, says, ". . . the human condition, fraught as it is with suffering and with the finality of death, demands interpretations that not only satisfy theoretically but give inner sustenance in meeting the crisis of suffering and death."

The *second* idea is the teleological argument, which is in fact an affirmation of faith. It begins from the assumption that this is a reasonable universe; that it has a purpose in it.

Consider the language of science. The fossils of the rocks and the various vegetable and animal species tell a story of countless ages devoted to the process of evolution. This process seems to be going somewhere. It looks as though it had a purpose. The end result of it all is man—human personality. In other words, our universe has lavished endless time and patience on the production of what we call personality. Does it make sense, then, to suppose that the universe after all this effort would suddenly turn around and blot out its most delicate creation? If you watched a skilled craftsman spending twenty years in fashioning a particularly fine watch, would you expect him to let it run five minutes and then crush it to bits under his heel?

Some people find consolation in the thought that, even if individual persons do not live on, personality itself continues, in that parents have children and they have other children and so the process goes on and on. But sooner or later, this world of ours is likely to become a cold, blackened cinder unable any longer to support life. Sooner or later, then, the last generation will come to an end, and the last person on earth will die. When that happens man's noble experiment on this planet will be over. And what will it have amounted to? Exactly nothing. But we believe our universe makes sense. All along the line it acts as though it were "up to something." And if it has gone to so much trouble to create personality, it is likely to take lasting care of what it has made.

A *third* reason is that in this life man can never become what reason says he ought to become, and what he is meant to become; and, therefore, there must be another life so that man may complete his development. If ever man is to become what he is meant to be, this life is not enough.

Within the whole range of the world's literature we find no more constant theme than this disparity between man's possibilities and aspirations on the one hand, and the narrow scope afforded them in the brief span of the present life. God never creates in us capacities for which there is no use. Man is equipped with his mind, with his intuitions, and with his love for something greater than this life.

This idea that we must be made for something more than we can accomplish on this earth is illustrated by the dragonfly. Someone tells of sitting in a boat one day, near the shore, reading a book. Suddenly he was aware that a big, black beetle (actually a nymph) had come out of the water and crawled up on the boat. He looked over the side of the boat and could

see there on the muddy bottom of the lake a score of these
ugly little creatures. Under the heat of the sun, the nymph
that had crawled out proceeded to die. Then a strange thing
happened—his glistening black shell cracked down the back.
Out of it came a shapeless mass whose hideousness was trans-
formed into beautiful, brilliantly colored life. Out of the mass
gradually unfolded four iridescent wings from which the sun-
light flashed a thousand colors. The metamorphosis complete,
this gorgeous dragonfly was soon dipping and soaring over the
water. But the body it left behind still clung to the boat. And
while the dragonfly happily explored its wonderful new world,
his relatives still plodded below in the mire. Were they aware
of the glorious creature flitting over their heads? Apparently
not. But out of the mud had come a beautiful new life. If
the Creator can work such wonders with the lowliest of creatures, should we not believe the human spirit will have another
world in which to expand, free from the limitations of the
body? Paul said: "This mortal shall put on immortality."

The *fourth* reason for our belief is that as Christians we
have faith in the character of God as set forth in the life and
teaching of Jesus. We begin with the faith that God is our
Father, and we are his children. If he is our Father, then he
cares for us. And if he truly cares for us, his concern lasts
not just a little while but always. We can say of him as had
been said of Jesus: "Having loved his own . . . he loved them
to the end." Then nothing, not even death, can take us out
of the Father's house or beyond the reach of his continuous
care.

It would be a heartless Father who would make us in his
own image, rear us into self-conscious sons and daughters,
develop our personalities capable of thinking high thoughts
and planning noble deeds, permit us to dream dreams of a
life that has no end—and then after a very few years snuff
us out as one blows out a candle. It is inconceivable that God,

who is supremely good, just and loving should allow those who serve him, offering their lives in his service, to perish as if they had never been.

But now we come to the question. What is this life on the other side of what we call death to be like? What kind of bodies will we have? How shall we put in our time? Frankly, it is not easy to extract from the New Testament any kind of clear and coherent statement of what happens after death.

The traditional view within Protestantism has always been that those who believe will share eternally the bliss of fellowship with God in heaven, while those who refuse his love are eternally separated from him in the misery of hell. This position takes human responsibility quite seriously but the notion of eternal separation from God for some men is hard to reconcile with the Christ-like character of God.

The Confession of Faith of the former Evangelical United Brethren Church, adopted in 1962, asserts in Article XII, "We believe all men stand under the righteous judgment of Jesus Christ, both now and in the last day. We believe in the resurrection of the dead; the righteous to life eternal and the wicked to endless condemnation." In the more recent doctrinal statement, something of the preciseness of this earlier confession is lost. There is little hint of future reward and punishment but a simple statement that we believe in the life eternal through the power of God's invincible love.

The fact remains, the matter of heaven and hell has loomed large in Christian teaching through the centuries and cannot be ignored. Yet the New Testament gives little information and what we do find there is symbolic suggestion. One symbol for hell is that used by Jesus when he made reference to the valley south of Jerusalem where the city's waste was dumped. This would remind us that hell is for those who have made themselves useless to God. Paul reminds us in Romans 6:23:

"The wages of sin is death—but the free gift of God is eternal life in Christ Jesus."

In general the New Testament seems to suggest that life after death is a continuation of life before death but on what is called a spiritual level. In this sense, eternal life is something that is given here and continues after death. If we grow in grace, in love and knowledge of God here, it shall continue afterward. If we are in rebellion here, then we shall continue to experience separation there. The goal of Christians is to do our best in fellowship here and leave to God what he will do for us beyond this earthly life. But we do insist that how we live here makes a difference in the world to come. Perhaps heaven and hell are appropriate symbols, or perhaps they no longer convey meaningful imagery because of the distortions associated with these terms in the Middle Ages. Nevertheless, we do believe that the quality of our life now has an eternal dimension. Jesus said, "Not everyone who says to me, 'Lord, Lord,' shall enter the kingdom of heaven, but he who does the will of my Father who is in heaven." (Matthew 7:21) We must therefore respond in faith and love, live responsibly and in obedience, and thus come with confident trust to the close of life knowing we can hear those beauteous words, "Come, O blessed of my Father, inherit the kingdom prepared for you from the foundation of the world." (Matthew 25:34)

Another view is described as conditional immortality. Immortality is not a quality of the human soul but a gift of God. The Scripture confirms this. "The gift of God is life eternal." Those who persist in opposing God's purpose of love cut themselves off from the source of eternal life and simply cease to be.

Another view widely held, is that of universalism. This says that all men will finally be restored to God. It rests mainly upon those New Testament passages which affirm the triumph of the God who does not desire that any should perish. It believes that God will find a way of reconciling all men without destroying their freedom.

Without attempting to describe the next life too precisely, here is what many United Methodists have come to believe Scripture and human intuition confirm.

First, eternal life begins now. Within this world of space and time we can enter into a relationship with God and it lasts forever simply because God is God. Human relationships can be and are broken. People drift apart. Death comes between. But to be in relationship with God is to be in a relationship which cannot be broken in death. When death comes, we simply move on to another plane but the relationship continues unbroken and uninterrupted.

Toward the end of his life when Jesus was trying to prepare his disciples for his separation from them, he said, "Let not your heart be troubled; believe in God; believe also in me. In my Father's house are many rooms." (John 14:1-2) That is really all we need to know. This present life is one room in the Father's house. The life beyond is another room in the same house. We don't need to know precisely where that room is, or what it looks like, or the kind of furniture it will contain. All we need to know is that it is a part of the Father's house, and his love and care are in control there as they are here.

Second, nothing short of eternal life is consistent with the character and purpose of God. But how is this possible? We know life only through a physical body and the body is mortal. Without a body, how can there be life after death? Actually, we do not hold to the Greek notion that the soul is a separate entity from the body and at death is set free to enter the presence of God. We believe the New Testament affirms that life after death is by resurrection, God giving us a body like Christ's glorious body. In fact, the first chapter of Romans reminds us that the resurrection-power is already at work within us and this is the meaning of "eternal life." It is something that starts now. And the interrelation of body and soul in this life supports the concept that in the life to come we shall have "spiritual bodies" and not be disembodied spirits. All of this, of course, is a mystery. If the child in the womb were capable of self-consciousness, it could not imagine what life would be like in the world into which it enters at birth. It is beyond the range of its experience. In similar fashion, our limited experience does not qualify us to understand all the intuitions, feelings, aspirations, hopes, and dreams that possess us. It is beyond what we can know or explain even though we are utterly convinced that there is "more beyond." But we do believe we will have a "spiritual body."

Third, this life eternal will be characterized by continued growth and development. For many centuries the Catholic branch of Christendom has taught the doctrine of purgatory. Protestantism has always rejected this and many Roman Catholic scholars have drawn back from some of the excessive interpretations. It was the abuse of this doctrine which moved Luther to initiate the actions which resulted in the Reformation.

United Methodists have rightly rejected the idea that salvation is something we win by our own merits. Eternal life is God's gift resulting from a relationship established with the heavenly Father in this life. Yet, I can't but feel that there must be some measure of truth in the idea that we will continue to grow, develop, abandon faulty attitudes of spirit, and go through a process of purification before we have the capacity to enjoy full fellowship with the Lord of all created things.

Obviously, we are in the presence of a mystery. There is much we cannot know in this life. Let us rest content in the knowledge that the Gospels come to a climax in the resurrection as a dramatic way of saying that it is God's will that we enter into life eternal. Jesus said, "Because I live, you too shall live."

This is all the promise we need for the present. Our duty is to receive in faith the gracious gift of God's redeeming love and yield our lives in joyous obedience to his will and trust the future to his care.

When Singapore fell to the Japanese in 1942, Mrs. Rogers Mulvaney, a Canadian, was working there for the Red Cross. Along with more than four thousand other civilians she was locked in Changi jail which had been built to accommodate four hundred and fifty prisoners. They suffered four years of crowding and hunger, loneliness and isolation, with no news of families and home.

As the first Easter approached, Mrs. Mulvaney went to the guards and asked if they might sing hymns in the courtyard on Easter morning. At first they were refused, but were finally given permission to sing for five minutes. In the presence of one guard they sang for five precious minutes, praising God for Christ's resurrection, the only hope to which they could cling. Then silently they marched back. But as Mrs. Mulvaney entered the passage-way, the guard stepped up, reached under his brown shirt, drew out a tiny orchid and placing it in her hand softly spoke, "Christ *did* rise." Then with a smart military about-face, he was gone. But Mrs. Mulvaney stood there, eyes brimming with tears, knowing that she and the others need never again feel forsaken. To know this is to know eternal life now.

12
LAST THINGS

"United Methodists, along with all other Christians, are a pilgrim people under the Lordship of Christ." This phrase from the Doctrinal Statement sets the stage for this paragraph: "We are called to proclaim and live out the eternal gospel in an age of catastrophic perils and soaring hopes. Humanity stands nearer the brink of irreversible disaster than ever before. Our reckless disregard of nature's fragile balances, our rush to over-population, pollution, the exhaustion of basic ecological support systems, the proliferation of nuclear weaponry go on unchecked. . . . At the same time, visions of a more fully human quality of life for all mankind haunt our imaginations and stir our aspirations as never before. . . . We who are caught up in this perplexing situation seek to understand our Christian faith and interpret it to others."

Do we know where we are going? Does history have a destination, or will it just come to the end of the line? Someone has defined history as "the succession of one thing after another." Taken seriously, this assumes that history is not going anywhere and has no ultimate goal or purpose.

It is reported that John Wanamaker once said: "I know half

the money I spend on advertising is wasted, but I can never find out which half." So we could acknowledge that much of our activity is unprofitable, but which part? Somewhere, we continue to hope, there must be a clue which will give meaning to it all.

Psychologists have suggested that the "western" is popular on television because it presents a world where wrong is black and right is white, and evil can be destroyed with a six-shooter. By way of contrast, our world seems hopelessly complex. A young minister, joining in a civil rights demonstration, was crushed beneath the treads of a bulldozer. The editorials in newspapers and magazines seemed uncertain as to whether he was a hero and a martyr, or a foolish and misguided young man. Little wonder that unwashed anatomies and weird costumes have become one of the symbols of our generation. They are the anguished protest against a society that is without apparent meaning. It reveals a desperate emotional need to find significance in man's historical enterprise. We are on the road, we are engulfed in activity, but where are we going? Is it to the end of the line, or to a destination? Man continues to play his part, but he wants to comprehend the play.

Most of the popular conceptions about the goal of history would suggest that things just go on until we come to the end of the line.

One such theory develops the idea that we will continue our "little round" until history reaches its end with an uninhabitable earth. Astronomers tell us that the sun will end human life. There is every reason to believe that, at some future point in time, physical conditions will no longer be conducive to the continuance of human life. While we may accept this as an inevitable reality, it tells us little about the meaning of life in its present form.

If history is nothing but going on in the same old pattern until this earth ceases to be habitable, then many of the things we do are without lasting significance and might well be omitted. But we hasten to add that the Christian need not capitulate to this theory about history with its inevitable cynicism which dissipates purposeful endeavor. Honest deliberation and prayerful searching will soon reveal the poverty of this answer.

Another possibility is that man's ingenuity will end human life before the sun can do it. We wait with a kind of vague anxiety for the thing to blow up. We now speak of "overkill." Russia boasts that she has the nuclear capability of destroying our nation one hundred and fifty times. By some ironic twist of reasoning, we seem to feel more secure because we can retort that we have the capacity for destroying Russia five hundred times! What difference does it make after the first time?

The late President Kennedy said the sword of Damocles hangs over the world. Damocles, who lived in the fourth century before Christ, once insulted King Dionysius of Syracuse. He was condemned by the king to attend a royal banquet and sit beneath a naked sword that was suspended by a single hair. We are under such a sword. It is swinging back and forth and the hair is getting more and more frayed with every passing day. Do you remember how we felt when we put our mines in the harbor at Haiphong? We waited, tense and anxious, to see what the Russian ships would do. We knew that, if they confronted our mines with a showdown, we might have come to the end of the line.

History's weariness with man's factionalism can easily lead to despair. The adherents of nihilism are apparently justified in their stance. In the preface of one of Winston Churchill's books, he writes: "I have called this volume triumph and tragedy, because the overwhelming victory of the Grand Alliance has failed so far to bring peace to our anxious world."

Man's self-destructive tendencies, most dramatically portrayed in his repetitive and meaingless wars, give credence to the conclusion that man's ingenuity will end human life. The Christian, however, cannot embrace this as *his* answer to the enigma of history.

If history does not end with the nuclear bang, there are those who think it will come to the end of the line in an existential whimper! There is ample confusion and tension in our present situation. There is an evergrowing assault upon our traditional social conventions. Morality seems to be established through a statistical equation. In blunt terms, this means that the adults are saying, as do the youngsters: "It's all right if everyone is doing it." There is a revolt against discipline which manifests itself in literature, art, drama, and music. There is a massive disillusionment with the old systems. The beliefs and practices of Protestantism, capitalism, and our political system generally are all under attack. The forces of social change are often beyond the bounds of moral and rational behavior. Rifle brigades, vigilantes, coercion, retaliation, boycott, intimidation—this is now the language of social ferment.

Are these tensions and expressions the birth pangs of a new and better society? Are they the death struggles of a history that is coming to the end of the line? Frankly, we don't know. History does inform us, however, that civilizations which tried to flee from their confusions and conflicts by absorbing themselves in the product of a sensate culture soon perished! This is dying with a whimper.

The *Cincinnati Post and Times-Star* carried a provocative article about western civilization, with particular reference to our own nation. It began: "The test of a great civilization is not its mechanical gadgets . . . it is rather a matter of imponderables, such as delight in the things of the mind, of beauty, honor, grace, courtesy, and delicate feeling." It went on to

illustrate how far we have drifted. Out of its many references
I shall select only one: "In one state, Nevada, we gamble away
more money in a single year (four billion dollars) than we spend
nationally on medical research. As a nation we spend thirty-
three billion dollars on gambling, more than we spend on the
entire educational system—kindergarten to university. We are
a nation whose bookies outnumber its physicians."

Does this sound like a society that should be preserved? This
frantic pursuit of the gambling craze grows out of our subcon-
scious conviction that, since nothing significant is ultimately
possible in history, we should take minor gratifications from
the perishing moments. Persuaded that the struggle is without
meaning, we avidly seek momentary escape and diversion.

I know there is an apparent irrationality about life. Lew
Ayers' death in *All Quiet on the Western Front* illustrates this.
After surviving until the end of the war, he is killed by the
enemy when he reaches out of a trench for a butterfly. Our
impoverished understandings, however, must not lead us to
search for meaning in the offerings of a society of over-
abundance. There is agony, but there can also be ecstasy. There
is high adventure if we move toward the rich affirmation of
human destiny. There is much more in the Christian answer
than the negative conclusions that history will collapse from
the fat of its own self-indulgence.

I think the reason for man's inability to arrive at an answer
is simple. An answer cannot arise from human logic because
our perspective is too limited. No one has experienced the
end of history. It is, therefore, impossible to reach ultimate
conclusions through the facility of the human mind. We turn,
then, to an examination of the Christian affirmation which
grows, not out of logic, but out of a profound declaration of
faith, based upon revelation. Here is our premise.

The Christian faith assumes that the historical process is
known in its entirety by God. He created both the process

and the people who take part in it. Furthermore, we believe he entered human history, and in the life, teaching, death, and resurrection of Jesus Christ revealed the significance of the historical enterprise.

This does not make much sense if we seek answers that are logical from our human perspective. The Christian declaration has always involved the dimension of faith as a response to the revelation of God. The gospel is a proclamation that comes to the world and some "get it" while others do not. To those who do, it is "the power of God unto salvation." To those who do not, it is a scandal and an offense.

The Christian view of history, furthermore, insists upon a linear concept rather than the hopeless cyclical repetition of "one thing after another." John Montgomery says that this understanding of history can be visualized as a "line which begins with creation, centers on the redemptive act of God in Jesus Christ, and finds its termination in sanctifying final judgment."

When we speak of creation, we are not primarily concerned with when and how this happened. These are questions for science to answer. Our statement grows out of a realization that God did it, and he did it that man might have a purposeful relationship with him.

From creation, we move to redemption. Man's rebellion broke the harmonious relationship which had existed between creator and created. "God was in Christ reconciling. . . ." The great act of self-giving love becomes the center of history. Love makes loss devastatingly real, because it lies at the very heart of life and death. The love of God, revealed in the act of the cross, displays the meaning of history and becomes the criterion for interpreting all other acts.

The Christian stance affirms that history has a destination in that it is moving toward a judgment that is final and perfect.

We do not often preach about an ultimate judgment. We are not certain as to what we should conclude from those scriptural passages which speak of judgment. We cannot avoid, however, the necessity of a final and perfect judgment at the end of time which will give history a direction, an ultimate meaning, and a destination. For the Christian the end of time does not hold terror, but anticipation. It is a time when inequity is set right. It is a moment of revelation when we shall understand the purpose of the struggle. It is the act wherein those who are in Christ will move from an incomplete relationship to one that is perfect and whole. By faith, we shall see the One who died to redeem us from the hell of our own self-seeking and who restored us to meaningful life which by definition is life lived in obedience to the law and will of God. In the meantime, the life which we live in Christ in the here and now will have the elements of change, choice, and confidence.

NOTES

NOTES

NOTES